GW00587442

THE SECRET CRICKETER

THE SECRET CRICKETER

ENGLISH CRICKET FROM THE INSIDE

First published by Pitch Publishing, 2021

Pitch Publishing
A2 Yeoman Gate
Yeoman Way
Worthing
Sussex
BN13 3QZ
www.pitchpublishing.co.uk
info@pitchpublishing.co.uk

A CIP catalogue record is available for this book
from the British Library.

ISBN 978 1 78531 986 0

Typesetting and origination by Pitch Publishing
Printed and bound in Great Britain by TJ Books Limited

Contents

Foreword 7

Acknowledgements 11

1. Starting Out 13

2. Making It. 33

3. Treadmill 68

4. Feeling Like A Rock Star 118

5. Country File 146

6. Pressure. 162

7. Coaching and Coaches 185

8. Leadership 210

9. Hiring, Firing, Earning, Recruiting and Moving 229

10. How Lucky Am I? 254

11. Around The Grounds 264

12. When the Treadmill Stops 274

Foreword

NOT ONLY have I spent the past 20 years pissing about on a cricket field, going from Travelodge to Holiday Inn and Nando's to Wagamama's, I have now written a book about it.

Being asked to become *The Secret Cricketer* has meant spending several months reliving some of the most sublime, but mainly the most ridiculous moments in a career I probably never thought possible.

When you see Cristiano Ronaldo enter the football pitch with his immaculate six-pack and hairdo, spare a thought for the unshaven, slightly tubby county cricketer who just put the wrong petrol in his club-issue Mazda and has to go and field for six hours. We're both professional athletes, but that's where the similarity ends.

But what a privilege it is to play such a unique sport, get paid for it and be surrounded by some of the best human beings you could imagine. Cricketers are a fascinating bunch, from the young lad who steals the changing-room beers to drink in his hotel room to the 6ft 5in quick bowler who emerges after 20 minutes in the ice bath to gasps of admiration from his team-mates.

When the two teams you are watching on an English cricket ground are absorbed in an intensely competitive struggle, regardless of the format we're playing, with a high level of skill on show, it is an example of elite performers at the top of their game. But behind the scenes you might find me keeping watch as my hungover team-mate is being sick in the toilets before going out and whacking a 70-ball hundred.

County cricket has its problems, and there are things in the game in England which most of the 400 pros making a living out of it would agree need to improve. Some have been issues throughout my near two decades as a pro. So, in these pages I've tried to offer some solutions on how we can do things better as well as taking you on the journey from junior player all the way to the top, well nearly the top. If the ECB want me to expand on some of my ideas, I am available for the usual consultancy fee.

At times it can be a pretty miserable existence, like every job really. You're out of form, the team spirit is crumbling, and there's no chance of winning a trophy. You're worn out, there's still six weeks of the season to go, and next up is a long trip to Durham. All you've got to look forward to is which service station to stop at.

But the good days far outweigh the bad. I have seen it all and met so many wonderful people; from the guy on the gate, to the umpires, supporters and dressing-room attendants who are part of the fabric of English professional cricket. When I sit back in 20 years, long since retired, and pick up this book, I'm sure I know I will still be grateful that I got to live this life for as long as I did. The county pro experiences far more good days than bad. I hope you enjoy reading about them for yourself.

Acknowledgements

IF YOU think you have worked out who I am by the end of this book, then well done. By staying anonymous, I've tried to highlight some of the issues in the game without worrying too much about upsetting anyone while bringing you the realities of life as a county cricketer.

But the trouble with a project like this is that you can't thank all the people who have helped you in your cricket career without giving your identity away. When the cricket writer who had the idea for this book came to me, I didn't need much persuading. He's helped me through the process and made sense of my thoughts through many Zoom calls. Thanks mate.

Thanks to Jane and Paul Camillin at Pitch Publishing for their support and belief in the project, to Duncan Olner for the cover design (we got there in the end), Richard Whitehead for his proofreading and generous feedback and to Alison Cooper, who professionally transcribed my ramblings.

The only three people who know I have written this book are my wife and parents, who have offered unstinting love and support from the day I first picked up a cricket bat and right through my career. And they've been sworn to secrecy.

This is for them, and everyone who loves county cricket.

The Secret Cricketer,
March 2021

1

Starting Out

I'M NOT sure how long cricket has been my life. I can't even remember the first time I held a bat in my hands or threw a ball at someone or something, it was that long ago.

Every young sportsman or woman has a support system as they make their way: parents, coaches or siblings. But if you are going to make it, that's all they are, support – not someone or something to blame if it doesn't happen for you.

You could be the most talented player in every junior team in your county, and even one of the best at your age in the country. You could be fast-tracked into the county second-team at 17, have the best equipment and access to great facilities and coaching.

Everything could be there for you to help you make the transition, but only you can make yourself good enough technically, physically and, most importantly, mentally so that when that opportunity comes you grab it.

All those things I've mentioned happened to me in my formative years. I showed an aptitude for ball sports very early on. I was playing two years above at the age of nine, facing loads of future Australian Test stars at 15 and playing county second-team cricket three months after my 17th birthday. I trained like a maniac, I watched my weight and I wanted it, I really wanted it.

In my mid-teens I had to overcome a pretty traumatic episode when probably one of the best-known coaches in the world tried to change my game so fundamentally that a few weeks later I turned up at games dreading the thought of even walking on to the pitch. Quite a few contemporaries who worked with him at the same time were ruined by his methods and their chance of a career in cricket disappeared. But I was mentally strong even then and got through it.

So here are a few things that happened when I was finding my way in cricket, how I approached and how I responded to different setbacks and challenges. I think for young players and parents they are still relevant now.

The right school – does it make a difference?

I coach kids occasionally nowadays, enough to get a sense of whether the development of young players has improved in the past 20–25 years. Some of these boys and girls have been educated in private schools, with the access to better facilities that gives them. Their parents are also happy to pay me £70 an hour to operate the bowling machine and encourage them along. Happy days. I have also worked with a lot of promising young players free of charge to try to help them in areas where they may not have had much help, so it's not just about taking a bit of spare cash off parents I can assure you.

In 2020, statistics showed that 43% of English professional cricketers were privately educated yet only 7% of the total school-age population in the UK go to public schools. That first figure is probably going to keep rising as more and more state schools sell off playing fields and fewer teachers provide cricket coaching after normal lessons. Those two things were just starting to happen when I went to school.

Does your school make any difference to your chances of making it? That figure of 43% suggests being privately educated does give you a decent advantage, but it still means more than half who come into professional cricket do so via state schools, universities or the club system.

The most important thing to remember is you are never more than a few miles from a cricket club in this country, whether you live in a city, town or a village. And there are coaches and volunteers working at local clubs who will be able to spot young talent and push it in the right direction, through their own contacts in county or Minor Counties cricket. So, is it access that stops young boys or girls being full-time cricketers? Are there advantages to living in certain counties? Does the cost of kit have a big impact on who can or who can't play cricket? The sport's lack of visibility is a much bigger issue, as has become apparent in recent years.

In my opinion, if you turn out to be good enough the opportunities to become a pro are the same now as they were when I started, whatever way you get there, and there are many different routes to the top. It is simple when you think about it. We still have 18 counties as we did 20 years ago, so we still have around 400 players who can make a full-time living out of the game. And that's not including players who play Minor Counties cricket for two or three days at the weekend and supplement their income by coaching in schools, often in the private system but sometimes for those enlightened state schools who still provide cricket facilities.

Of course, you've still got to have talent. When I speak to parents, some are anxious that the 'pathway' their kids might end up on in a county's junior or academy set-up will not improve their chances, that they will get swallowed up in 'the system' like hundreds of others.

I have one response to that. If they are still in the system by the age of 15, they are – technically at least – almost certainly going to be good enough to progress. The rest is up to them. If you cannot drive yourself to be among the top 400 or so in the country then you should think about doing something else. If you are good enough, you will score the runs or take the wickets that get you to professional level. The rest, particularly being mentally strong, is up to you.

This is something that I have heard repeatedly over my career. When I mention that I am a professional cricketer I often hear the same sob story, 'I played for my county at 16, could have made it but the selectors preferred x or y.' That's fine, but if you didn't make it because one coach didn't like you, I can categorically say you wouldn't have survived the continual setbacks that would have come your way between the ages of 16 to 19.

This is common across all sports. I understand and have sympathy for those who have opportunities taken away by injuries or illness. But, if you were good at 16, and it would have taken another two or three more years of really hard work and sacrifice so one day you could play in front of 30,000 at Lord's, don't tell me some idiot in a tracksuit stopped you.

Professional cricket is 40 people fighting for one career. Work as hard as you can, give it everything, and if you don't quite make it be proud that you gave it a right go. Don't sit in a bar and tell me you were/are as good as me and all my peers when we have worked for everything we have achieved. Don't tell me about your 3-60 in the under-15 club final and expect me to say you're unlucky to not be playing for a living week in, week out.

Don't just play cricket

I have a sibling who was also a very good sportsman, which is not unusual. It certainly helped me no end. He probably could have played professional sport as well, but he decided it wasn't for him. He still loves sport and has been my biggest supporter throughout my career.

My dad was also a keen sportsman and helped me so much by just being there, never pushing me and allowing me to make my own mistakes while enjoying the ride. We regularly share a beer and laugh about the times he was so nervous he could barely speak, or would hide in the ground holding a random bit of metal or wood he had found walking around the boundary while watching my last successful innings and decided it was a lucky omen!

So many of my peers had expectant parents and that is the hardest thing I have seen and continue to witness in sport, not just cricket. Plenty of parents are wonderfully supportive and I don't see anything wrong with a parent who will do whatever is needed to help their child to achieve their dreams. Mine largely left me alone, apart from taking me everywhere. Others may provide this, but also pay extra for specialist coaching or training.

It is the ones who try to live their lives through their kids that cause the problems. These kids grow up to be adults that end up resenting the game and the miserable existence it gave them. If a player makes it to the top, it is down to their drive and hard work. When you are out there in the heat of battle, it is you who is accountable. No one else.

There aren't too many players who make a career in cricket who have been pushed so hard they end up hating the game. Encouragement from a parent can be so important. A player who makes it and enjoys it hasn't been pushed too hard. That's important.

Playing a wide range of sports was key to my development. I see so many kids being pushed away from other sports so they can focus on doing their gym work and whatever the strength and conditioning coach decides they want them to do at that time. I can safely say that playing a range of sports helped me develop physically for cricket, and also gave me an all-round enjoyment of sport in general.

To see young kids doing all these drills makes me wince a little. Go and play tennis or squash, build your hand-eye co-ordination in a fun and free environment. Once you turn pro you are going to be a cricketer 365 days a year. There will be no time to play other sports, so let young players loose and allow them to develop naturally in a variety of sports.

A lot of coaches won't do this as it isn't something they can control. I have worked with enlightened coaches who encouraged tennis in the winter, or some five-a-side football, and others who would barely let you leave the house unless it was to go to the gym or running track.

Fitness levels in English cricket have gone through the roof during my career. There are still plenty of players who don't quite fit the mould of what a professional athlete should look like, but remember cricket is fundamentally a skills game.

The fitness side should always have a relevance to the sport, and this is something games like squash, tennis or badminton can really enhance, as well as providing the competitive element. It also gives players a break from the monotony of going to soulless gyms in the basements of county grounds, trying to motivate themselves.

Have some heroes – even if you can't emulate them

I was encouraged to play by a coach at my local club who saw me throwing a ball about and made sure I joined a team and started my cricket journey there and then. These people are invaluable to the game and I have huge gratitude to the amazing volunteers and organisers who allow kids to play the game in clubs all over the country.

The media love to show pictures of England's newest star when he was a freckle-faced kid picking up his first trophy at the end of season awards. Or they dig out a nice headline in the local paper and find the coach at his first club who put him on the road to stardom. At that age it's nice for the ego, being the best at sport also makes you popular at school.

When I was growing up cricket was still on terrestrial TV so access to your heroes was readily available. Mine were Michael Slater and Merv Hughes. Slater was the Aussie opener who lit up the 1993 Ashes by trying to hit every ball to the boundary. I even had the same Gray-Nicolls bat and pads as him, handed down from my older brother. I liked Slater, he was a bit rogue, and I guess the equivalent

Englishman at the time was Robin Smith, someone else I liked. Big Merv was *the* big personality in the Australian team at the time. His moustache and the way he seemed to bully the England batsman. If, like me, you wanted England to win it was horrible, but fun to watch at the same time.

I was a cricket badger. When *The Cricketer* magazine came out every month I'd cut up the articles and rearrange the layout so I was in all the headlines. I used to pore over the reports and scorecards in the paper every day.

I once bunked off school to go and watch a county match which was televised, and the headmaster spotted me in the crowd and sent the deputy head to our front door the next day. They got short shrift from my mum, 'TSC wants to be a cricketer and he'll learn more watching cricketers than sitting in your classroom' – and slammed the door in his face.

These days it might not be considered healthy by parents for kids to be so obsessive about something. Just be as supportive as you can. If I'd wanted to be a bookseller or a flower arranger my parents would have driven me to the library or the garden centre. Most parents are the same.

It helps to remember where you came from

I would say I had a fairly privileged childhood; my parents did everything to make sure I was happy, and I will be eternally grateful to them for this. I went to the local comprehensive, I sat on a park bench getting pissed and I'd go to the youth club where, fuelled by cheap cider, I'd act a bit lairy. My school reports all said the same thing, 'Loads of energy, bright spark, could do better.' I got enough A levels and my parents always provided for me, but most of my gear was handed down by my brother and for years I carried my cricket stuff around in a travel bag.

Many years later, if I was struggling for form I would think back to my formative years when I started falling in love with cricket as a way of reconnecting with the game again. Sometimes, I would drive miles just to walk around the outfield where cricket started for me, remembering games I played as a kid. I've had a lot of setbacks in my career, as every professional sportsman does, but I've never lost my love for the game. That definitely helped me play for as long as I have.

One thing which makes me laugh is when the next big thing returns to his club after playing in his county's second team and struts around like he is Ben

Stokes. It is crap, and I get how opponents end up spending the day abusing them and wondering how the fuck they can act like that.

It is a bit embarrassing. I have seen county pros turn up for club games in a lease car which cost them their whole monthly wage wearing their county shirts with their name on. Why? They are massively insecure, but to them it is a way of showing everyone they are good. I try to motivate young players to get really stuck in; what better way to earn respect and support than by giving your all in a game of club cricket and helping your team-mates. I have seen so many county players who get sent back to play club cricket then act like complete pork chops. Give a little back and help the club players, maybe even stick around for a beer afterwards because you never know when you might need their support. Actually, you probably need it now because while you're helping take the covers off on a Saturday you could be playing at Lord's and enjoying sticky toffee pudding for lunch!

Stick at it

You'd probably be reported to the authorities if you did this now, but I remember one summer when I was 14 or 15 playing for 30 successive days out of 32. Any game going, I would put my name down for. I would turn up and play for other teams, even though I knew I would be batting at No.11 and not bowling, just fielding.

A couple of times when I realised I wouldn't be batting again there would be tears. 'I just want to play,' I'd bawl at the coach. I still see him now, and we have a laugh about it. It wasn't nice but it taught me some really good lessons:

Be patient
Work hard
When you get your chance take it or don't moan
Don't be a prick

At 17, I broke into the club's first XI and was playing against county pros in the league on a Saturday but only batting at No.10. The coaches realised that was too low and moved me up the order. I never made any threats about leaving. An older player made way and a new guy came through and that was the way it happened, through evolution and good communication.

Speaking to the coaches at my old club now, I realise how much things have changed. A lot of lads aged 14, 15 or 16, especially those who have been privately educated and are told they are the best thing since sliced bread, can't accept a hierarchy that means when they turn out for their local club on Saturday that they might have to play in the second or third team and perform consistently before they get a chance in the firsts.

Instead, they tend to piss off to another club, even if the facilities and standard of cricket are lower just so they can say, 'I'm in the firsts, I score loads of runs' and feel good about themselves. What they don't realise is that the opportunities to be spotted, nurtured and perhaps play age-group cricket for your county become less frequent the further down the leagues you fall. No coach ever looks beyond the top division of his county's league to spot players who may have slipped through the system. And, of course, playing against good players, whatever age you are, improves you.

Train smart

When I was young, if I wasn't playing cricket or another sport I'd go running to improve my fitness. I should have been lean and mean given all the exercise

I did but I was conscious even in my mid-teens that some of my contemporaries were more ripped than me. Stupidly, instead of training smarter, I thought I needed to lose weight so I could develop a six-pack. Some days, all I ate was lettuce sandwiches. Thankfully, understanding of the importance of a balanced diet is an area of the game which has improved markedly. Back then coaches were so uneducated about it. They could not tell who was naturally fit, or if someone needed to reach his absolute optimum just to pass a basic bleep test.

Nowadays, a lot of cricketers still struggle with body image. For every pro sitting in the weights-room after a session posting a picture of his ripped torso on his Instagram feed another is hiding his belly folds under a towel in the corner of the dressing-room. I'll return to this topic later on because I think it can become an issue.

Setbacks can be good for you

I was lucky. Apart from the odd tearful outburst when I didn't get a bat, I coped well with setbacks from a fairly early age. I'd be pissed off, like everyone is, when they get out for nought or their bowling is taken apart, but it didn't put me off. I think it was my inherent love of cricket, and everything about the game, which gave me that resolve. Nothing was ever given to me. I didn't mind playing in my brother's oversized pads or waiting until my gloves and boots literally fell apart because I'd used them so much before they were replaced.

If there is one thing I have learnt in the past 20-odd years which I believe is fundamentally more important than anything else in terms of a player's development, it's that if you're going to make it to the very top, or even the level just below, you have to have overcome setbacks in your development, whether that is getting dropped, having a shit season (not a few bad games which happens to everyone) or a serious injury. As I alluded to earlier, mine came when a top coach nearly ruined me. I'll talk about this more in the chapter about coaching.

After I became a professional, I saw lots of youngsters follow me into the county's professional squad who had a gilded career at junior level and who were clearly talented. And then, when they came up against players who were as good as or better than them, they struggled to cope.

Once you leave the schools and junior system it's a different game for a 19-year-old who is used to having his arse wiped and his ego massaged for ten years by his coach, whether it's in the academy or at school. We've all been there to some extent. But as soon as you join a county as a pro, for every young player there are 15 experienced ones desperate to assert himself. You have to learn quickly how to deal with this shit.

I hear about gun players in academies all the time. And all I want to know is how they react to their first big setback. During my career, you can count on one hand the players who have made serene and uninterrupted progress from their first game of organised cricket all the way to the top and a long England career. There are always pitfalls.

In county cricket everyone knows each other. It is a small world and I am always interested when I hear about the next big thing. There is always the player who bursts on to the scene, gets all the press attention and sometimes attracts a few nice sponsorship deals before they have even hit a ball. They come in and make a few pretty fifties in their first season and everything looks rosy. Some get picked for England

and flourish, but most disappear very quickly never to be seen on a county ground again.

When a player becomes a pro it is the first step on the way to a long and rewarding career. The biggest challenge comes when they are faced with the gnarled veteran who has been around for 25 years. A dependable old seamer can play with a 19-year-old like a cat with its prey, tossing him and turning him until finally he puts the youngster out of his misery by whacking his front pad. This is when you find out if the player has more about him than just a glittering junior career against his private school peers.

I like to see how a young player bounces back from these early experiences. Do they become the bitter player at his club, moaning to his opposite number in second team matches that they should get more chances? Or do they take their medicine, work hard to overcome the problems and aspire to come back stronger and more prepared for the big bad world of professional cricket? These are the players I watch out for and believe could reach the very top, and if not have long and rewarding careers in county cricket.

My own setbacks did leave mental scars because all of a sudden I doubted if I was technically good enough. Fortunately, a couple of key people in the county I ended up at thought I had enough talent, allied to my enthusiasm and dedication, to work with. I was told I *could* be a pro, and that was enough to make me work hard enough to *become* a pro. There are a lot more of us who were like that when they started than not.

I know without any doubt that the setbacks I have encountered during my cricket career will help me for the rest of life; I know I can deal with them, and I am stronger for my experiences.

2

Making It

WAS I READY when I made my County Championship debut? Don't make me laugh. There I was, preparing to go back to college for another year to continue my education (cricket and non-cricket) and, all of a sudden, an injury to one of our senior pros, a call from the coach and a boy enters a man's world. I had suddenly gone from being one of the best players in my club team, someone who has churned out runs in second XI cricket thinking he might be getting somewhere, to this environment. Trotting down the pavilion steps with some genuinely world-class players in front of me (I was too scared to walk out ahead of anyone else) while a few others in the opposition dressing-room glanced up and wondered 'Who the fuck is TSC?' I looked around and tried to take it all in.

There were people watching. County cricket fans like seeing new players come on to the scene, it intrigues them. They consider it a badge of honour to be able to say, 'I remember seeing x make his debut' when said player goes on to have a stellar career. And at the back of the pavilion in the press box, I could just make out half a dozen writers ready to pass judgement. Years later, I remember discussing my debut with a journalist who covered my county home and away for the local paper at the time. That fact alone tells you how long ago it was. Anyway, I asked him if he remembered what he told the other reporters about me. He was at least honest. 'To be honest TSC, I didn't even know whether you were a batsman or a bowler. I'd hardly heard of you.' Needless to say, I made a negligible contribution to our performance which ended in a heavy defeat.

I was buzzing inside, of course I was. But I had done nothing in terms of consistent performances to justify this promotion. It felt like a one-off, or in the best-case scenario that there might not be another opportunity for a while. I was 18 years old and I knew fuck all about professional sport.

I later discovered that the captain and coach took a punt on me not because I was the most talented option available to them but because they liked my attitude. But that can only get you so far of course. So how do you make that transition from academy cricket to playing a first-class game and, eventually, making a career out of cricket? And what advice would I offer to those about to set out on the same journey myself and thousands of other county pros have taken?

University challenged

University cricket is much maligned and in recent years funding has gradually been reduced. I think it is a good system, one where players can have a few years studying whilst remaining in a semi-professional environment and return in the early summer to their counties. Look at how many players have come through into the county game via this route in the past 30 years.

Look, I know it does not prepare you fully for the county game. There's a reason why county players put up with the delights of the Parks or Fenner's in freezing-cold March and April to fatten their averages against student attacks in matches that are deemed to be first-class. When your county's committee are discussing your contract offer at the end of the season, only the sharpest will remember that 200 of your 1,200 runs came against Oxford or Cambridge Universities. Students are on a hiding to nothing in these games, but they do get exposure to good-quality cricket, often in testing early-season conditions. You might not do very well, but it's a great experience, and as a stepping-stone from academies or even good standard club cricket there is nothing better. And when you play Oxford or Cambridge, there tends to be a few students sitting around the boundary smoking pot and pretending to study who can offer free advice on the best place for a night out.

Some universities offer a real focus on cricket and allow students to train, play and study at the same time, often in that order of priority. Some of the university teams I have played against have had a whole host of guys who went on to have successful county and international careers. The coaches are well regarded in the game and it gives players a few extra years to improve, while also making sure they have something to fall back on if cricket doesn't work out.

More importantly, that period between 18 and 23 is when you really grow up, you become an adult.

There is no sadder sight than seeing a 20-year-old scrapping for his future after two years as a pro when they weren't quite ready. Pack them off to university for a few years to get some life experience, and they will be in better shape to walk straight into county cricket.

I have always thought that life experiences are key, whether it is going to university, getting some work experience outside of the game or pissing off overseas to play grade cricket on your own in the winter. So many players love the home comforts of their academies and weekly schedules, but when it ends there isn't anything to show for it.

I would love to know the exact stats, but I would bet that universities have produced more county players than academies in the past two decades. It is a far better finishing school for would-be pros than second-team cricket.

Train smart

It took me a few years before the penny dropped after I kept getting niggling injuries. Not enough to stop me playing, but enough that when I did, something always ached.

Then it dawned on me. 'Why should I prepare the same way as a 21-year-old 6ft 5in fast bowler?' By the middle years of your career, you realise that you need to train smarter, doing drills that work for you and not anyone else. I'm convinced that players who realise this earlier than I did, say in their early 20s, will have a longer career – as long as they can convince their coach that at that age they know what is right for them.

When you are young a competitive instinct kicks in. If a team-mate runs a mile in 6min 30sec, you want to do it in 6min 15. If they bench press 100kg, you want to do 110kg. Then when your body rebels you realise you need to wise up. Some players hate training, but are you really going to drop a player who takes ten minutes to run a mile but then goes out and gets you 1,500 Championship runs or takes 70 wickets?

It's a real bugbear of mine. Fitness is important, but often the investment in it doesn't correlate to its importance. Players like Ben Stokes and Jos Buttler have become better players because of the fitness levels they attained. They are not deemed better at cricket because they are fit.

I see that one-size-fits all approach still prevalent in academy cricket these days. Lads, the copy and paste culture does not work, like so many unscientific things in our game. It just seems to take cricket longer to find that out.

Analyse this

These days, I would say that analysts and the work they do probably helps a player more than a technical coach. It's certainly the case once you've played for a few years.

They can help in so many ways. Before every game they will come up with a detailed breakdown on what to expect at each venue. If you're about to play at Northampton for the first time in a couple of years they can tell you your runs scored split against right- and left-armers, how many times you have been out in a certain way there and whether you have scored more runs in the first or second innings.

For coaches this sort of detailed data is invaluable when assessing potential new signings, and especially if you are comparing players. And for an individual, the right targeted information can give you a massive confidence boost.

I'll give you an example. For years, when we used to play Middlesex our team's batsmen would wonder how they would contend with Steven Finn, who got the ball to bounce because of his height and could regularly touch speeds of 90mph-plus, even in white-ball cricket.

I used to face him a lot when he took the new ball and I always thought Finny was one of my toughest opponents, especially in white-ball cricket. Then one day, after I'd got out to him after I'd scored only 20 or so, the analyst came up to me and said, 'Unusual for you to struggle against him.' I thought he was taking the piss, but then he showed me his laptop and it turned out that I scored 9.8 runs an over on average against him. I'm pretty sure Finny wasn't aware of that because in my experience fast bowlers tend to have selective memory when it comes to batsmen who dominate them. But the next time I faced him I knew the chances are I would do well – the stats said so. Going into any battle with any bowler with that mind-set really helps. So, when I carved him over backward point for six in his first over I knew it was par for the course. I say I scored quickly against him, but he also had my number on a few occasions and he has had a brilliant career. It may be that because he had the ability to hit me in the head I went after him a bit more than most, but it does show how what we perceive as our weaknesses can be way off, and how some simple analysis can change your thinking.

I remember coming up against a bowler who I thought knocked me over for fun and, in the first innings, he bowled me for fuck all again off a massive inside edge. I went back to the dressing-room complaining to anyone who would listen that although this guy had the wood on me, it wasn't because he was too good for me but just down to bad luck. Then I asked, out of curiosity, how many times he'd got me out and nearly fell over when the analyst said, 'Well actually, you average 65 against him.'

The Steve Finn stat got me thinking. I asked the analyst for a breakdown of my record against bowlers over 6ft 3in, who invariably got extra bounce. It took him a bit of time, but they did show that I consistently scored well against bowlers with extra pace and bounce. I used to love facing Steve Harmison for instance, because like Finn I didn't need to play forward to him. I could sit in, wait for him to bowl with just a touch too much width and smash him over backward point or gully.

And, of course, in Test cricket every side has a couple of bowlers with those attributes. True, they might not give you too many deliveries where you could free your arms, but facing quicks consistently did make you concentrate more. Which got me wondering whether if I had got an extended run as a Test batsman – say ten games on quicker pitches – I might have done well. We'll never know, but it made me feel better for quite a while against tall, fast bowlers who have won the Ashes.

But for every surprising stat that the analyst might come up with, there are players against whom you know your record is crap and no amount of dressing up the figures can change that.

For instance, Keith Barker used to get me out for fun. He wasn't tall, didn't get the ball to bounce disconcertingly and he was never quick. You would think if I could score heavily and consistently against Finn and Harmison, then Barker would be a doddle. But he bowled wicket-to-wicket with a bit of shape on the ball, and rarely bowled anything loose. So, you end up chasing runs and taking more risks. When I started doing that against him he knew he had me. And I probably did as well.

Broaden your world view

I remember popping down to the nets at my county towards the end of the year. I was at a stage in my career when my coaches knew that asking me to start preparing for the new season in October or November was a waste of time. After a long summer playing in three formats, you are physically and mentally knackered, more so the older you get. You need a change of scene and a complete rest from the treadmill.

What surprised me were the number of junior pros working away busily at their game. Nothing wrong with that, but it's an easy environment where everything is done for you and the coach is always on hand – metaphorically at least – to wipe your arse.

Two weeks after I signed my first contract – a one-year deal worth £8,000 a year incidentally – I was on a flight to Australia to play club cricket for six months during the winter. Looking back, I don't think I would have had the career I ended up having had I not done that. It improved me as a person and as a player more than any number of winter net sessions could ever do.

I turned up in Australia, got picked up by a bloke from the club I was playing for and we drove to the car park at the ground where this old banger was parked up. I was told that would be my transport for the next five months. On my way to the house where I was staying the car broke down. I had no mobile phone and I hadn't a clue where I was except I knew I was somewhere in Australia. In situations like that you have no choice but to think for yourself. I somehow managed to retrace my steps back to the club, found someone there who got in touch with the club president and he came and collected me and got the car towed away to a garage where I waited until it was repaired. Straight away I had to solve a problem.

Even after that little escapade, things didn't get much better during the next few weeks. A fortnight in, I hadn't scored a run, I didn't know anyone and because my team-mates thought I was a crap player they made little effort to get to know me and I was barely earning enough money to feed myself. I would go back to my room and bawl my eyes out.

The easy thing would have been to fly home and, to be honest, 25 years later, I don't even know why I stuck it out. Shame and embarrassment at having to go back, probably. But a couple of weeks before Christmas I finally got a hundred and things clicked. Of course, I missed my family and friends. I remember watching *Love Actually* at the cinema and desperately wanting to be home for the festivities. I was still homesick.

It's a tough environment because you have to prove yourself. Until you get a score Australian club players tend to think that their first-grade cricket is better than the English county system, and that most young English professionals are soft. You are a nobody over there, they don't give a shit. It's a hard school, but you learn to adapt and survive. And once you get some runs, you can start giving a bit back on the field and in the bar afterwards.

I started to enjoy a regime of work, cricket, gym and beach. I got really fit because I had the time and access to the practice facilities 24-7. I worked hard on my game so that when I came back the following March I felt like a different player. Just as importantly, for my own self-confidence if nothing else, the perception of me among the other players and coaches at my county altered too. They could see I had changed, physically if nothing else. I looked like a professional athlete and at a crucial time in my development I was playing hard, competitive cricket where every innings was important.

In the end I went back to the same club for the following two winters and, later in my career, I played for clubs in New Zealand and South Africa. As I got older and became a better player, going overseas felt less pressurised and became a much more rounded experience. I took my girlfriend with me, I made more time to make friends and to explore the country. They were wonderful life experiences; the cricket almost became secondary to everything else.

Over the years, young players have approached me and asked what it's like to spend the winter overseas and of course I recommend it. But when I tell them what to expect – and these days it's a lot easier because communication is so much better – quite a few are put off. They reel off a list of demands which I think are totally unrealistic. Some only want to go for three months between January and March; they want a car guaranteed and decent accommodation; they don't want to work behind the bar or help mow the outfield or coach the kids, they just want to practise and train and spend any down time on the beach.

Most clubs tell them to fuck off. Too right. What makes it such a rewarding thing to do is discovering things about yourself and your character; it's not just a cricketing experience, it's a life experience. I would recommend it to any young player.

It is part of a wider issue I see in the game. I'm not sure if current players in their late teens or early 20s have that determination and drive now. In modern society, and I think sport reflects this, players seem to get rewards and gratification without having to work as hard as previous generations. There seems to be a softness to them, a belief that the only validation they will ever need is from their peers through social media. We will come on to that later.

Second rate

Some of my fellow professionals might not admit it because it will not be good for their careers, but second-XI cricket in England is a complete waste of time and has been for years. If it is going to continue, it needs to be reformed.

The only period during my career when I felt it had any relevance was when I was coming back from injury and needed a couple of matches, or when you played in a joint game where two counties made up one team and played another split the same way.

Those games tended to be reasonably competitive and the standard higher because neither team contained lots of career triallists – lads who basically refused to accept they were not good enough to be full-time professionals – or players from the academy.

When I got into the first team on a regular basis one of my aims was never to play second-team cricket again. It didn't happen, sadly. Everyone gets injured and after a period out of the team you must get back on the horse somewhere. Coming back to it years after I'd last played in the seconds was the worst experience ever. Shit cricket for three days, playing with a bunch of kids or triallists with no affinity to the team whatsoever and who were only interested in how they performed. Which I understood totally, even though I knew it was wrong.

After that, if I was ever asked to play by the second-team coach I refused. And to be fair the head coach backed me up because he knew a couple of decent net sessions were much more beneficial.

I played in one such split-team game when one of my team-mates had trialled for all four counties who had supplied players, a professional triallist if you like. He had played with the majority of lads on both teams. He went around the circuit doing this for a couple of years, picking up appearance money, despite knowing that the number of triallists signed as pros among the 18 first-class counties each summer is in single figures.

Second-XI cricket has always been crap and it's got even worse over the years. Back in the early 2000s, county staffs tended to be bigger, with 24 or 25 players. If everyone was fit, you sometimes couldn't even get a game in the seconds and in that scenario it was the guys who needed cricket more than most – young players finding their way – who tended to miss out on selection.

I do pity second-team coaches. What a job they have, especially if there is no hope of promotion to the first team because the head coach is doing a good job. He has to deal with embittered senior players who have been dropped and would rather regroup away from the game for a few days than play in the second team, which is seen as a kind of punishment. Then there are youngsters who think they have outgrown the second-team environment and should be in the first team. Coaches have to make sure everyone can get to the ground if you have youngsters who don't drive; pick up the scorer because he needs a lift and ensure the food for the players is of a sufficient standard. And then there are the triallists. *In fact, perhaps it's the best finishing school for any coach when I look at it like that.*

One of the main reasons why it's so poor is because of where most games are played. When I started, my local club would host a couple of second-team matches for the county and they pulled out all the stops. They would prepare two good wickets in the middle and they would let the players practise on the square on pitches as good as the ones they would play on.

Nowadays, most small clubs are not fussed – it's become a hassle. Why make all that effort when you could hold a junior festival for three days instead and make loads more money over the bar from the parents?

It is only among counties who have built their own ground for second team and academy matches, or who taken over a club ground and invested in the good facilities for the same purpose, when you know you will be playing on a decent pitch. What possible benefit is there to English cricket in playing a second-team match on a crap wicket where neither team scores more than 150 in either innings or half of the team is made up of triallists? Second-team cricket is not going away, and I can't claim to have a long-term solution, but I do think there are ways that it can be improved immediately.

Pitches first. Why not prepare wickets that specifically challenge a player's skill set? Why can't we deliberately prepare surfaces that, say, turn on day one or play successive games on the same pitch, so in the second game it spins? In my experience, spinners in second-team cricket might as well not bother turning up. They usually have to bowl on flat, batsman-friendly surfaces with tiny boundaries to protect or an underprepared wet shit heap that's over in a day and a half. It's a thankless task.

The aim of second-team matches should be to prepare your top four batsmen to play county cricket. Who cares if the No.7 can score runs in that environment? Your opening bowlers ought to be able to bowl two or three six- or seven-over spells at the same pace as the first and your spinner should be able to bowl the opposition out on the last day.

It ought to be about creating pressure situations. Why not limit the number of overs in the first innings? I played in one game when I was coming back from injury where the opposition, who were going for the title, did not declare their first innings in a three-day game until after tea on the second day. I got so bored by mid-afternoon that I walked off, claiming I had a headache. I got changed and went home.

Create scenarios that are going to challenge the skill set of all those involved. I would even go so far as to say that once he has organised practice before play that the coach leaves and lets the captain run things. The only players over 25 I would play in any second-team match are the captain, who ideally would be an experienced pro with no agenda whose remit is solely to provide guidance and an honest assessment to the head coach on whether player A or B is ready for the first team, or a player coming back from injury.

Once a player over 25 is stuck in second-team cricket there is very rarely a positive outcome. Second-team cricket is a development tool, nothing else. Who remembers who won the Second XI Championship or either of the one-day competitions? No one takes any notice of the averages because the gulf in standard is vast. I'd be embarrassed to say I was a Second XI Championship winner, but I have seen quite a few players with that proudly on their CV and their LinkedIn page.

But for every radical like me there are, I'm afraid, plenty of players who feel comfortable in that environment. They score lots of runs or take loads of wickets, but then they cannot perform when they get the chance in the first team. So, they go back to the seconds and the cycle repeats itself. You end up with a situation where there are guys in their mid-20s on county staffs earning £25,000 a year who have played less than 20 first-team games, but have been a professional for three or four years. No county pays you more for good performances in the second team. The best you can hope for is to get a year's contract extension and the same ridiculous cycle starts again.

The cap can fit

The capping system has largely disappeared now from county cricket. Increasingly, players have specific contracts related to the amount of red- or white-ball cricket they play, but I still believe that it is only when you are capped, or get an equivalent reward from your county, that you feel you have established yourself as a professional cricketer who, with a bit of luck, can look forward to a decent career in the game.

The biggest benefit is in your wage slip. My money went up 50% when I was capped three years after joining the staff. When you were on a relatively small salary, which most players are for their first few years, that makes a massive difference. That's the biggest perk, but there are others. You get to park nearer the dressing-rooms for starters. It doesn't sound like much of a reward but try lugging two cricket bags and a load of dirty clothes stuffed down your cricket trousers and tied at the bottom (incidentally, this is the most ingenious thing a lot of players can manage) for 500 yards in the pissing rain. It is not much fun.

It's also a prestige thing. You feel different the first time you walk on to the field as a capped player. You are wearing the jumper and cap which signifies you're capped and straight away there is more respect from the opposition.

It's odd, because in terms of your ability you are no different, but you've got some games under your belt, you've turned 40s and 50s into a hundred a few more times or two-fers have become four-fers more regularly. For the generation of players like me who came into the game in the first decade of the 21st century, getting capped was the remaining ambition if you knew you weren't going to play international cricket.

When I moved county I didn't get capped and it did piss me off, especially when an overseas player, who had maybe only played a couple of international one-day or T20 games, joined us and got his cap ahead of guys who'd churned out 15,000 runs or taken 300 wickets, even if it wasn't for that county. By then you're earning good money anyway so it's purely a prestige thing. But honestly, decisions like that cause more friction and create resentment than a lot of other things in dressing-rooms.

It helps to have a profile

Away from the game itself, the biggest change in cricket during the past 20 years is how cricket is presented in the media.

When I started the bells-and-whistles TV coverage you see on Sky Sports now was still in its infancy and social media didn't exist.

So, in order to get a bit of a profile and give your career a boost, not only had you to perform on the pitch but you also had to hope cricket journalists wrote something nice about you. It will seem a quaint ritual now to players coming into the game, but for years the first thing you did when you got to the ground or the hotel breakfast-room on an away trip was scan the reports in the papers to see if your name was mentioned in the match reports. I know plenty of players who would cut out articles or even references to themselves in articles. One former team-mate kept a massive scrapbook so detailed that some of the cuttings would be one sentence in the middle of a paragraph where he got a favourable mention for a shot he played.

On many occasions back then players who were pissed off with what had been written about them would march up to the press box to confront the author. These are called Press Box Incidents, or PBIs, apparently. I remember one game at Cardiff where the slanging match between our captain and a journalist went on for 30 minutes and could be clearly heard out in the middle. Very amusing. No one likes being criticised in any forum, but I always thought, because county cricket is quite a close-knit community, that it felt worse in our sport than others. It sometimes felt like being insulted by a member of your own family.

Sussex used to have a very talented all-rounder called Robin Martin-Jenkins. On the circuit most people thought he was good enough to play for England, at least in one-day cricket. He bowled a heavy ball and in the lower-middle order he could score runs quickly. When his father Christopher, the very well-respected cricket writer, covered Robin's games he would desperately avoid mentioning his son in his reports in *The Telegraph* or *The Times*, even if he had done well, for fear of being accused of nepotism.

And when he didn't do so well, you could almost feel professional jealousy creeping into the reports of Robin's performance from his father's rivals on other papers. Poor old Robin couldn't win really. He still had a fine career and his late father must have been very proud of what he achieved, but if Christopher hadn't been the eminent figure in the game he was I think Robin would have played for England.

For the last decade or so, though, TV has been the most important platform for county players who think they can play international cricket. It 100 per cent helps to play well in front of the Sky cameras and any player who tells you different is talking complete crap. I remember once playing a pull shot in a T20 game that sailed into the crowd for six. My next thought wasn't 'I fucking nailed that' but 'If this game had been on Sky, that shot would be replayed 5,000 times.'

You see it all the time now, a fairly nondescript T20 game on a Tuesday night at Leicester in front of a few thousand fans. Some young lad who no one has ever heard of apart from cricket badgers plays the shot of his life which is shown on the Sky Sports cameras. Twelve months on and the social media manager is replaying it again and again, saying how good he is. The player gets a bit of a strut on, gets an agent and demands a new contract and a pay rise. Try dealing with that as a head coach in the modern game. Largely on the basis of that one shot, it seems he suddenly became a player the media, and specifically the Sky commentators, are talking about. It can happen that quickly and on such relatively little evidence. If Mike

Atherton or Nasser Hussain, who I think are the two Sky commentators most county pros respect more than anyone for their opinions, give you some good raps it can do wonders for your self-esteem. It does mean something.

As in any other walk of life, there are good commentators and bad ones. Those who have players reaching for the mute button on the dressing-room TV tend to think they have spotted a flaw in someone's technique and spend the next 20 minutes giving said player his own bespoke coaching lesson during a live broadcast. The worst ones are the commentators who try too hard. Most of you will know who I mean, the ones who make you turn the volume down as they spout some over-reaction to the most mundane event just to make a name for themselves. Others, like Atherton and Hussain, know the value of silence and to allow the picture to tell the story.

Being a very good player in a different era like Dominic Cork was means your opinion should carry some weight and sometimes the more analytical commentators can come out with theories which are very interesting. But a lot of the time if I'm watching cricket on TV – which, to be honest, is not very often – I turn the sound off. And I am like the vast majority of pros, I hate watching myself.

But there are a few who adopt a completely different persona when the cameras are around. I have seen players who aren't even playing deliberately warming up or practising behind the presenters so they are in shot in the hope that they might be asked to give a brief interview about how their recovery is going, just to keep themselves 'out there' and in the public eye. Others will go out of their way to say hello to the commentators and be especially friendly, usually in the mistaken belief that if they get out for a duck or their bowling goes around the park those commentators might be more forgiving.

The downside to all this is when players change the basics of their technique based on something a commentator mentions, like when a batsman who falls over to the leg side too much, or keeps nicking off. I have seen players head to the indoor nets during a game to practise a shot or tweak their technique based purely on the assessment of a commentator who might be watching them for the first time.

The social side

I consider myself lucky in a lot of ways, not least because for the majority of my career I wasn't scrutinised on social media.

I have Twitter and Instagram accounts. It's a platform I like because I genuinely find some of the stuff which is written about me, especially after I've done badly, quite funny. It amuses me to think of people hammering away at a keyboard and expressing pent-up frustration in 140 characters when they've just seen on Cricinfo that I got out for a duck or my four overs in a T20 have gone for 46. And, of course, they have never met me.

But in recent years I feel social media has become a big issue in the game, a hidden problem if you like. Most counties offer training on how to use the tool responsibly, but for youngsters who know little else about mainstream media other than social platforms getting that valedation on Twitter or Facebook when they make runs or take wickets seems to be becoming as important as the performance itself.

Look, every player likes reading nice things about themselves, but when you're out of nick and every game seems to be a struggle, scrolling through rather less complimentary stuff on your social media feed, often from the same people who were praising you to the hilt a few days earlier, will only add to your problems.

I have mentioned this to a lot of young pros, but most ignore you. For every Zak Crawley, who doesn't go anywhere near social media, there are many young players living their professional life through its prism. I genuinely believe that it will not be long before counties have to employ specialists specifically to help players deal with the pitfalls of social media and the problems it can cause to mental health. With its prevalence in modern life, they could one day become just as important as a coach who feeds the bowling machine in the nets.

I'll be honest. When it first started I was a bit like that myself. I sought validation on social media when I performed, but quickly learnt to keep away from it when I didn't do so well. But then I befriended a family who watched my county where father and son would regularly play cricket on the outfield during the interval. I gave a few tips to his son who wanted to be a batsman, I was nice to the boy's mum. I even gave his father my number so he could text me if he ever needed tickets, which I'd then leave on the gate free of charge.

Then one day, a team-mate took great delight in pointing out that not only had the father shredded me on Facebook and Twitter after a poor performance, but that his ten-year-old son had as well! That night I deleted my Facebook account and never went on it again. I only wish a few more players had the gumption to do the same. It's hard enough establishing yourself as a professional cricketer without letting things which you can control get out of control.

In a spin

England's issue with spin bowling once again came into sharp focus during the series against India in early 2021 with the county game inevitably getting its share of the blame because most of our best players struggle against spin. It certainly seems that an England Test or white-ball win is celebrated by the ECB with little reference to where the players learned their trade, but a loss or poor performance invariably leads to criticism of county cricket mostly from people who hardly follow the domestic game, far less watch it on a regular basis.

The ignorance that surrounds the domestic game in England baffles me sometimes. The ECB control it – no one else. They choose the schedules and the competitions that are played and most importantly when they are played. The county game is constantly berated for being 'cosy' or lacking ambition. Let me tell you, on a day-to-day basis there is a constant commitment to improving and playing the best cricket among country pros. But when you spend 24 days in 27 playing with travel on top what do people expect?

When England won the T20 World Cup in 2010 we should have been celebrating the influence of Loughborough as a centre of excellence, of central contracts managing the workload of the top players but also the 400 county pros who are working hard every day in English domestic cricket.

When England became the top ranked team in the world in 2011 the players were nurtured through our domestic game and earned places at our national academy. Where did players like Ian Bell, Matt Prior or Andrew Strauss return and find the form that got us to that no.1 place?

The fixture list which pushes Championship cricket to the margins of the summer means that we rarely encounter any turning pitches apart from Taunton and Chelmsford during the height of the season, never mind April, May and September when most four-day cricket is played. Here's a few ideas of my own which might help us prepare better to face quality spin in Asia.

- Use a Kookaburra ball in April and September which is less likely to swing and seam.

- Play County Championship games during The Hundred. How many red-ball players are twiddling their thumbs during the peak summer months, who are not involved in The Hundred or play one-day cricket? There will be enough players on a county staff to play a Championship game which has meaning with the same points at stake, even if the team isn't necessarily full of a county's best players. It would incentivise clubs to also look at the best players in their academies and give them some exposure and forget about, for those weeks at least, meaningless second XI matches.

- Why not play two games on the same pitch and make it a prerequisite that each team plays two specialist spinners during this fortnight? This would also take a bit of pressure off county squares.

- Let's not penalise teams for preparing spinning pitches while allowing green seamers which are just as much of a lottery for batsmen. Be consistent and have criteria for pitch preparation. What about stipulating that the grass on the ends has to be a maximum of 3mm and thus creating a bit of rough? So many games are over in two days with 40 wickets taken by seamers and there is radio silence, yet Somerset or Essex are put under the microscope every time the ball turns. I always loved playing at these grounds because you felt you had to play really well to score runs. Whether it was people around the bat and big spin at Taunton or Simon Harmer bowling round the wicket with a leg slip, it focuses the mind and examines your technique but at least you have a chance. You play with a Dukes ball on a wet pitch at Worcester and it's a procession of batsmen nicking crappy half-volleys. This doesn't translate to the demands at the top level so we need to change our way of thinking.

I get the whole 'it will lose its integrity' argument but the reality is the domestic game is here to serve the international arena, it is here to provide players with the platform to excel and help England become the best team in the world. Why shouldn't the ECB exert some control over how the players will be tested in regards to pitch preparation in particular?

There is no coincidence that two of the three spinners in the England team play for the same club which highlights the huge difference between being a slow bowler at Somerset and, say, Durham. In the final Test in India arguably our most accomplished batsman apart from Joe Root, who is head and shoulders above anyone else, was Dan Lawrence. Now remind me. Who does he play for and who might he encounter in the nets on a regular basis?

We have some good spinners who never bowl in April and May. I think the way we regulate our pitches must be better and the England head coach and captain should be able to influence the domestic structure, so it helps create the players they need who are capable of playing in all conditions and on all surfaces around the world. Australia now use a Dukes ball in certain rounds of the Sheffield Shield. Now why would they go and do that?

3

Treadmill

LET ME take you into the inner sanctum of any professional sports team – the dressing-room – and tell you a bit more about the daily life of a county cricketer.

County cricket is a treadmill a lot of the time and any player who says differently is deluded. I'm sure a few of you are thinking, how the fuck can I call it a treadmill. I get to travel around the world playing cricket and are paid quite nicely for it. I wear my discounted Oakleys and drive a nice new Mercedes, whilst mere mortals pay £15 for the privilege of turning out for our club on a Saturday.

It's the same as supporters shouting abuse at footballers who expect them to love every second because they are getting paid so well. If you were going to pay me £60k a week I'd happily spend the week in a cage until it was time to run around for 90 minutes. Cricket is different. Unless you reach the Holy Grail of playing international, IPL or Big Bash franchise cricket regularly, the chances are you are on a solid salary, playing contract to contract whilst trying to make sure you've got something lined up for when you retire.

That is worth remembering if you are watching a 24-year-old struggle to realise his dreams and start slagging him off on social media. He might seem fair game as he's perhaps living out your dream, but the reality is that he's probably earning £25k a year with nothing to show for it when he is spat out by the system. And it's a dream he might only follow, sometimes through no fault of his own, for a couple of years.

I have seen so many really nice lads come through academies and do OK for their county, but then the next bright young thing wanders in, there is no room in the squad for them and all they have got to show for their endeavours is a cupboard full of used kit. The leased Mercedes has to go back, they might have to leave their rented flat near the ground and go and live with their parents again. All this while they are still in their mid-20s. If you're going to slag off anyone, direct your ire towards guys who have been around for maybe a decade and are still not getting anywhere, whilst remembering that even though they might be earning £40k they still won't be retiring to their yacht in Marbella when it's all over.

County cricket takes its toll mentally and physically, it is a fucking long 11 months. Winter training can be arduous and at times fairly boring, and once the season starts it does not seem to stop. You look forward to a precious day off like someone in a desert who spots an oasis in the distance.

That is why winning the County Championship is still the Holy Grail for county cricketers. It is 11 months of running in the cold, being prodded by the fitness coach and facing or bowling thousands of balls. You play 14 four-day games over six months and the satisfaction of winning is as big as it gets. No other title in English sport takes as long and more effort to win. The toll it takes on you is huge. Most of us have sleepwalked their way through the last month of the season in a daze, dreaming of October and a few weeks of drinking and eating what we like and sleeping properly before the treadmill starts turning again in mid-November.

The major upheavals in the domestic game have taken time. It was only in the early-1960s that professional and amateur players stopped coming out of separate dressing-rooms. When I started there were still a few counties where the second-team players changed in a separate room from the established pros. Twenty years ago at the majority of grounds you practised on the main square because there was nowhere else to prepare. At some you still do.

Now, most clubs have outstanding practice facilities, including indoor centres. At the start of the century not many counties had those. When it rained you were confined to the dressing-room or forced to do desultory laps of the outfield if you had some energy to burn off and weren't interested in playing cards or doing the crossword in *The Times* or *Daily Telegraph* (the county cricketers' favourite newspapers since time immemorial incidentally).

Now, as soon as it starts raining, I would say more than half of my team-mates will head to the indoor nets to work on something and the rest to the gym. That is once they have stopped scrolling down their phones to check their social media feeds. There doesn't appear to be a lot of time anymore to sit down and actually think a bit about what you're supposed to be doing and whether it's working for you and the team. The one thing I miss is just sitting around having a chat, for which I mostly blame mobile phones. I fucking despise those things in a dressing-room. Fortunately, during play they are banned because of match-fixing protocols, but they have become a massive distraction.

Anyway, let me take you on a tour of England's shires and offer a little behind the scenes look at the minutiae of county cricket. I have been asked a lot of 'what's the best?' and 'what's the worst?' questions by curious people during my career. Here are the answers.

Changing rooms

The worst? The old dressing-rooms at Derby were awful. Hardly any room and only one toilet for about 18 blokes. So, when you came back in after a stint in the field, you'd end up pissing in the showers. One lunch break ended far too quickly and as the bell went the coach started panicking. Six blokes were desperate for a piss, but with one toilet taken by the physio having a shit it meant we all slid into the showers in our spikes, and this was a very slippery tiled floor. We all had to piss in the plug hole and get out on to the field before the umpires sent a search party. As we ran out the physio emerged with the paper tucked under his arm wondering what all the fuss was about.

After three or four days, particularly if it was warm outside, the place had that heady cocktail of sweat and stale piss, except for a brief period 30 minutes after the close of play when a dozen or more different deodorants briefly sweetened the air.

The best place to sit in a dressing-room is always the corner, because there are usually two pegs and a bit more room. These days the pokiest dressing-rooms are at Leicester. I don't think players carry any more kit around than they did when I started, but once 18 blokes put their gear down at Grace Road and the physio sets up his couch in the middle there is room for nothing else. I've lost count of the number of team-mates who have stubbed their toes, trodden on something or stumbled and fallen arse over tit trying to negotiate their way in and out of the Leicester dressing-room. On a number of occasions, I've had to tell the 'white-ball specialist' who is just here to bowl a few yorkers at lunch to move his kit out sharpish. You would be amazed how much kit someone who is just there to roll a few out during lunch brings. When you are sitting on your rucksack trying to get your pads on and he is spreading his kit all over the shop there is a strong urge to take his brand-new bag of unused batting kit and lob it out of the window.

Chelmsford is another place where things haven't changed much. If you played there in the middle of summer, you were guaranteed to lose a few pounds just sitting in the dressing-room for 20 minutes. It is like a sauna, so fucking hot. I remember once our physio getting out his thermometer and it read 50 degrees! Imagine how unpleasant that was with all those blokes and their kit in a relatively small space. You also have to share the toilets and showers with the Essex boys. Communal facilities. It's like being back at school. Hardly the right environment for elite sport, but that's what makes it such a fascinating game. How many people who turn up at the Oval on a Friday night to watch the Surrey superstars play T20 know that the next day these same players will jump into a few sponsored cars and spend the next four days sweating in a boiling hot changing room getting abused by David Masters?

You always look forward to going to grounds where there has been some new development. Then you arrive at places like Taunton and Cardiff and realise they have built the spacious new changing-rooms south-facing so from 10am until 5pm the sun is shining on the windows all day and it's boiling hot. At Trent Bridge, on the other hand, they are north-facing and even in the height of summer it's always freezing.

But there is one thing that makes Nottinghamshire and Surrey stand out from the rest. Both counties have always employed amiable dressing-room attendants to look after your whims, even if you're an opposition player. You leave at the end of a day's play and the dressing-room is a complete tip, but when you return next morning it's immaculate. It's so nice that players then think they can take the piss out of these guys, especially when it comes to laundry. There used to be an amazing bloke at Taunton, but he was so good the miserable bastards at Somerset sacked him as he made it too nice for us. From then on it was one towel for the entire week. Not pleasant.

I've known players horde filthy kit for a couple of weeks in the knowledge that they've got a game coming up at the Oval or Trent Bridge where the attendant will wash it all for them. Usually, if you hand it to them at the end of play it's all ready for you next morning. Lovely. It's like having your own butler. Not just kit either, blokes will happily hand over a bin bag full of shirts, socks and pants as well and they will be laundered overnight.

The form at the end of the game is you have a whip-round, each player lobs a fiver in and you give the guy £50 or something. But there are always a couple of tightwads who'd get washing done every night, including their personal stuff, and won't leave a penny. It's embarrassing. It's probably the biggest out-of-pocket expense I've had in my career – throwing in extra cash from my wallet for the dressing-room attendant because a few of my team-mates think washing their shit-stained smalls is all part of the service, and a free one at that.

Dressing-room attendants gain legendary status around the grounds, and rightly so. I've spent a lot of time sitting with them and finding out more about them. They do a lot of it for the love of the job, so when you walk into their rooms and you see the messages, shirts and kit from the best players in the world it's no surprise.

These are the people that make county cricket tick, and my one wish is that everyone treated them with the respect they deserve. These guys will do anything for the players and they always do it with a smile. A signed piece of kit or a donation of your old kit so they can pass it on to their local club is the least you can do.

It's fairly normal, certainly at the end of a game, for loved ones and kids to come into the dressing-room to celebrate or commiserate with the players and staff. That's fine. But I draw the line at pets. Imagine Jose Mourinho walking into the dressing-room to give his team talk and Harry Kane is sitting there, stroking his poodle.

Well in cricket different rules seem to apply. I've seen dogs roaming around dressing-rooms, pissing on the floor, in a player's kit bag and once even trying to cop off with another dog! You're trying to get ready to bat in a T20 and there's a dog barking because his owner has buggered off for a few minutes. Not ideal preparation.

Keeping it clean

Personal hygiene is important in any team environment, but more so in cricket because you can sometimes spend five days with the same blokes, sharing what is often quite a small space. Kit smells, no matter how many times you hang it on the balcony of the viewing area or leave it to dry on the edge of the outfield. You can't get away from that. With all that gear around, some of which has been used a lot, there is going to be a pong emanating from most players' kit bags. In that environment, personal hygiene becomes even more important.

Yet you would be shocked at the number of players who, after a long day in the field or, having batted for hours and hours, come off the field and get changed without showering or even having a wash. It can cause big problems for team morale. On average I reckon it's at least a couple in every team.

Normally a word or two from a couple of team-mates does the trick. Something along the lines of 'you fucking stinking mate, go and have a shower'. But when that doesn't work, more drastic measures are called for. I have seen players literally lifted off their feet, frogmarched into the showers by two or three team-mates, stripped naked, covered in Lynx Africa (not theirs of course, because they don't bring any) and forced to stand under the shower for ten minutes. How a grown adult can be so insensitive that he ends up being forced to have a shower like he is a naughty five-year-old baffles me. On many occasions, as we packed the car to go from one venue to the next at the end of a game, I've refused to drive a smelly team-mate until they have had a shower.

No one says anything if a player new to that environment waits until everyone else has finished before going to the showers, as long as he has one and looks after his personal hygiene. It's just about being considerate to your team-mates.

Then there are those players who insist on wearing the same kit, whether they are playing or training, for days on end. Sometimes it's unavoidable to go out and field with a grass stain on the knees of your trousers on the final day of a four-day game because you've run out of clean stuff at the end of an eight- or nine-day stint on the road, but when this goes on for three or four days something has to be done.

Once, our attendant was so fed up looking at a pile of a player's festering kit in the corner of the dressing-room that he gathered it up (with the permission of the coach by the way) and lit a small bonfire round the back of the building, while the player was in the field. He must have noticed because when he came back in, he asked where the smoke was coming from. Eventually he twigged and always had spare kit from that day onwards. It's not as if we don't get enough kit, most of it free.

I was lucky. My sponsor always provided new kit when I needed it, but countless times I have seen fungus growing on socks and mould on pads. Caps and hats were the worst, because you would sometimes wear the same headgear for seven or eight years. There is a certain amount of pride in wearing the same battered cap for a while, because of the happy memories it might stir, or because it has brought you some luck. The Australians' baggy green is the best example of this, worn until they literally fall apart. But caps are small items. When players wear the same shirt or pants for days on end, that is a problem.

Final word on the showers. The best facilities are at Lord's because they also provide expensive Molton Brown toiletries. A nice touch. For years, as soon as you arrived there you made a beeline for the showers to fill your wash bag with free Molton Brown stuff, knowing it would be replenished the next day. In recent years they've started to attach it to the walls like they do in hotels. I ask you. The MCC should hang their heads in shame.

Flat out

Going back to dressing-room attendants. As well as spending half their day loading up washing machines, they will undertake all manner of odd jobs for players during a day's play. Going out to get an ice cream, visiting a cash point or filling up a player's sponsored car with fuel takes the piss a bit, but most accept it's part of the job. Going to the airport to pick up or drop off family members is another of their regular unpaid tasks, although filling the fuel tank up and not getting reimbursed by the player when they do so is not on. But it happens.

By far the worst job they have is clearing up the mess in a rented flat when the lease runs out and the player has lobbed the keys in his direction and pissed off at the end of the season. I heard so many horror stories from our attendant over the years about this that one day I went with him after our overseas pro, who had a bit of a reputation for, shall we say, not leaving things as he found them, moved out of his flat.

Christ, I have never seen anything like it. I half-expected piles of unwashed crockery and cooking pots encrusted with grease lying in a sink half-full of fetid water and I wasn't disappointed. I wasn't too surprised either that I had to walk across a carpet that made a crunching sound underfoot because it hadn't been hoovered for months, or even that the player concerned was too lazy to walk to the communal bins at the back of his block, so he left five months' worth of rubbish piled up in black bin bags on the balcony.

The biggest horror story, though, was in the bedroom where instead of washing his bed sheet he had simply put another one on top. We peeled off ten disgusting bed sheets about an inch thick in total. Who has ten bed sheets, you might ask? No one does but this guy had gone out and bought eight bed sheets because we found the Dunelm wrappings discarded in the overflowing bin in the corner. The pillow had a brown ring where the outline of his head had lain. You get the general idea. Cleanliness was not next to Godliness for this bloke. Mind you, he did score over 2,000 runs that season so he was forgiven.

The inner man

I'm going to buck the trend here. Most pros will say the best grub on the circuit is at Lord's, and it is still very good. Shame they got rid of the machine that dispensed refills of Coke, Fanta and Sprite all day though.

But in my career the best place to eat was Derby, before they moved the kitchen when they did up the ground. It was like being in a five-star restaurant. It wasn't haute cuisine by any stretch, but the meals were home cooked by people who clearly loved their job and cared about what they served up. The biggest challenge for years at Derby wasn't normally what you faced on the pitch, but in the dining-room and wolfing down three courses in time so you could have at least five minutes lying down in the dressing-room letting your food digest before going out again. When I started, at most grounds you could have soup and a bread roll, a proper roast with three or four veg and pudding afterwards. Then the sports scientists got involved and for a few years everywhere you went – even Derby – it was grilled chicken or salmon and as many visits to the fucking salad cart as you could manage, with not an apple crumble or jug of custard in sight. But in the last few years it has gone back the other way a little bit. I like to think it's because grilling chicken and salmon and splicing open a lettuce or six wasn't stretching the imagination of the chef enough.

One of the best places to be if you're batting all day is Worcester, but if you're going to fill your face with homemade cakes from the Ladies' Pavilion make sure you get the dressing-room attendant to fetch them for you. A couple of us once tried to sneak over there only to be stopped in our tracks by an urgent text from the coach, who spied us through his binoculars while watching the cricket and dragged us back to the dressing-room.

Players genuinely look forward to certain away trips because they know they will be well fed; it's probably the thing that they judge the quality of grounds on above everything else. Who is that bothered if the wicket is a minefield if you can walk in at 9am and there's a plate of sausage and bacon cobs on the dressing-room table or, to keep the sports scientist happy, salmon and avocado? Club and festival grounds tend to be great at laying on breakfast. The trouble is that club wickets tend to be substandard so the game is usually over quickly and you might only spend a couple of days making the most of the hospitality.

Most dressing-rooms have toasters with unlimited supplies of bread, butter and jam. Quite a few fast bowlers will eat nothing else all day if they know they've got a long day ahead in the field, then wonder why they put on weight. When I started it was still possible to chow down on a plate of sandwiches and cakes at teatime, but not now. A wrap and a banana are usually all there is time for in 20 minutes. Shame.

But for every ground with a good reputation for food, there are places where it seems to be very low on the list of priorities. Hove used to be shit, although it has improved, and for years the best food at Hampshire was the chips, because Shane Warne used to get a plate delivered to him in the home dressing-room every day.

But consistently the worst is Northampton. For a few years when they had financial difficulties there was even a rumour on the circuit that the chef had been pressed into helping prepare the wicket because they were so short-staffed. Maybe he did a job swap with the groundsman because I remember one Championship game there where we ordered in food every day from Nando's. Some players nipped out one day when we were batting and walked to the Abington pub down the road from the ground and had steak and chips. One of my team-mates did venture into the dining-room and a couple of hours later threw up what he claimed had been a Lancashire hotpot.

When it's that bad it can actually depress you. After a long session in the field, especially if it's hot, it can be dispiriting to think as you go off for lunch that the only edible, thing on offer are the bananas and sandwich you picked up at Tesco Express on the way in. But there is still no better feeling than bowling a side out and knowing the next day is a batting day so you can have breakfast at the hotel, maybe a couple of sausage baps when you arrive, three courses for lunch – and then a full-on dinner in the evening with your team-mates.

One of the great things about playing professional cricket is the fact we eat out pretty much six nights a week; even during home games we might pop out for some food with the lads because we can't be arsed cooking at home. This is where you get to spend time away from the pressure of the changing room with your mates, you create the bonds that last a lifetime.

Sometimes you are all just feeling the heat a bit and need to wind down.

On one away trip a few of us went out for a nice meal, not just to Nando's or Wagamama's, but a proper restaurant as a treat. We were struggling as a team and once we ordered one bottle of wine, that quickly turned into about eight and we staggered out of the restaurant four hours later having put the world to rights. The next morning we were in a bad way but cracked on and won the game and the season improved steadily after that. Take note coaches. When times are hard, let the players relax and let their hair down. Extra nets aren't always the answer.

In the early years of my career most counties had a tradition when about 15 minutes before stumps the dressing-room attendant or 12th man would head off to the bar and return with a tray full of drinks, some alcoholic and some not and you would sit around for a few minutes having a drink and chatting about the day's play. Now, if you want to rehydrate you are pointed towards the water or isotonic stuff in the fridge. To be honest, when you have been at a ground for the best part of ten hours you are desperate for a change of scene, even if it's just the hotel. As a result, the post-play pow wows have all but disappeared unless the game is finished and you have something to celebrate, or there is the need to hold an inquest.

The best place to field

In the slips, 100% no doubt. No running around, a bird's-eye view of the pitch you are going to be batting on later, and the chance to talk complete nonsense for hours on end. I would say that the average three- or four-man slip cordon, wicketkeeper and gully fielder spend 10–20% of a day talking about the game in front of them and the rest about subjects ranging from one of the lads having a 'date' in the hotel bar last night to three down in *The Times*' crossword.

During my career, I have taken part in slip-cordon competitions to guess the number of people wearing hats who would walk into the pavilion during an over; how many tomatoes the bloke sitting next to the sight screen had in his lunch box (three: we checked when one of us had to go and field the ball at fine leg); which umpire would fart next; and the number of journalists in the press box actually watching when the next ball was bowled (one out of seven). Then there was all the usual nonsense five young blokes standing within a couple of yards of each other for three hours might chat about. One of the most enjoyable fielding periods I remember came before a members' Q&A which was being held at lunch. We weren't playing great cricket at the time, so to see the queue forming at 12:30 was one of the funniest things I have seen. The only thing missing was a picket line and the elderly punters singing protest songs.

Next time you hear a spectator shout something, look at the slip cordon. Inevitably, we'll be repeating what they say for our own amusement. If someone farted as a bowler was at the top of his mark, you'd pray that the edge didn't carry to you. Inevitably, when that happened, most of the cordon couldn't keep a straight face and certainly wouldn't be able to hold on to a thick edge.

And here's a thing to remember next time you are at a game looking through your binoculars wondering what we're all laughing about between deliveries. You would be surprised at how much we notice and can hear in the crowd. We could be laughing at you.

All the gear …

Yes, I know we're very lucky. Once you become an established pro you won't have to buy a single item of equipment ever again – with one exception. The one thing specialist manufacturers don't tend to make is footwear. Unless you have a sponsor, you have to buy your own trainers and boots. And boy do we make them last, especially if we've had some success in them. At the start of my career, I was in awe of the experienced pros who would carry around a mini tool kit so they could carry out running repairs, particularly to boots, to make them last the season.

I was with one of the bigger bat manufacturers for years and as well as free gear they paid me a couple of grand too. Nice work if you can get it. I'd go to their workshop during pre-season training and take away eight or nine bats, some of which were made to my specifications. I'd try all of them in the nets and in pre-season games, keep the best three or four to use during the season and send the rest back.

But on many occasions over the years I've gone to their workshop, picked up a bat off the shelf that I wasn't supposed to have, liked it and taken it away and scored runs with it. For batsmen it's an instinctive thing. You only have to hold a bat in your hands for a few seconds to know if it feels right, and that applies as much to a No.11 as an opener. At the end of the season most players will sell their surplus bats to mates or players at their club and donate the money to charity because they have a lot more runs left in them for recreational players.

On some occasions I have picked up a team-mate's bat and it has felt really good in the hands. The problem starts when you go and use it and get a shedload of runs with a bat made by a manufacturer who isn't your sponsor. I remember one year using a bat in those circumstances and scoring more than 2,000 runs with it. I didn't use another bat all season. Unusually for me, I even kept it and wrote a breakdown of the runs I'd scored in the various competitions on the back of the blade. There wasn't any comeback from my sponsor, either because I wasn't on TV much or didn't have my picture in the papers playing a glorious cover drive with the maker's name prominent. So he hadn't noticed or, more likely, he knew it went on and wasn't bothered. After all, it's only superstars like Joe Root and Ben Stokes who are likely to shift big quantities of bats that they endorse to clubbies and youngsters.

A bit higher up the food chain, where there is a lot more media exposure, changing bats can mean peeling off the existing sticker and replacing it with your own sponsor's logo. Believe me, this is not an easy thing to do because the glue is very strong. It can be done, but it takes hours and a lot of patience, a commodity most cricketers don't have when it comes to equipment. In recent years manufacturers have got wise to this little ruse and have started to mark bats for the superstar players with an imprint on the side of the blade. But it still goes on.

It is a lot different if you are sponsored by some of the smaller companies who will often sign players, normally youngsters playing for their local county. For example, Chase supplied a lot of Hampshire players for years to showcase their equipment. Most big firms aren't bothered if you break a bat, but some of the smaller set-ups can be a bit tight. If you break one of theirs and it's not beyond repair you have to send it back. Sometimes there will be a limit to the amount of free clothing a player can have as well. When you get a bit more established your agent will normally be able to sort you out a deal with Gray-Nicolls, Stuart Surridge or the like.

Which brings me on to what you do with your kit at the end of the season.

One size doesn't fit all

It's a sight you see at cricket grounds regularly, sometimes at the end of a game or more often at the end of the season. A couple of dozen people, mostly (slightly over)grown adults, hanging around the dressing-room while players throw used shirts, training tops, even jockstraps or pairs of gloves at them. Then, at the first game of the following season, you see the middle-aged bloke who grabbed your one-day shirt walking around in a sportsman's-fit top with your name on the back and his beer belly poking out of the front.

Professional sports kit as a general rule should not be worn by non-professional sportsmen, especially anyone over the age of 40. This should be enshrined in the Laws of Cricket, or at least be a ground regulation. Put on a fleece for fuck's sake. If the shirt is framed and hung on their lounge wall then fine, but seriously, what possible use are a pair of batting gloves you've worn for three months except to grow fungus and cultures?

After it has been worn kit stinks, but these individuals are quite happy to put it straight on and applaud you and the team on to the field while wearing it as a way of showing their support. You see it at a lot of grounds where you have to walk through a group of them. Trouble is, if it's a bit warm by the time you go out for the afternoon session this group of well-wishers are starting to collectively stink. Somerset, Hampshire, Glamorgan, Nottinghamshire, Durham, Leicestershire, Worcestershire and Northamptonshire are the worst culprits for this. It's a sort of wall of BO to get through before you enter the field.

It's different with kids. They don't tend to hang around at the end of the season waiting for your old kit anyway, but quite often I'll see a youngster batting or bowling on the outfield and give him something to stop him being crushed in the rush of middle-aged men when our star batsman flings his Royal London Cup shirt out of the dressing-room window. If that kid subsequently walks around the ground with your old T20 shirt that's fine by me. Any player who says they don't get a buzz out of people wearing a shirt with their name on it is a liar. Except when it's worn by a slightly overweight man and your sweat stains under the armpits are still visible, never mind his.

Actually, thinking about it, there is one thing more embarrassing than someone wearing your old kit who doesn't have an athlete's body and that's when you chuck a shirt towards the baying mob at the end of the season and it lands untouched on the ground because no one wants it. It's never happened to me, but I've seen it happen to other players and they have never lived it down. It lies there until the ground is empty then the player concerned picks it up as he's leaving, shoves it in his pocket and hopes no one has noticed. But someone always does.

Getting somewhere

During my career there has been a major shift in the way players travel to away games. When I started you drove everywhere. Some players had sponsored cars, but when the Inland Revenue started taxing it as a benefit in kind most counties had to change their agreements with local car dealers and a player's name was no longer plastered on the doors.

There are a few team-mates of mine for whom this was the ultimate indignity. Never mind that they hadn't scored a run or taken a wicket, the thrill of driving around town and people occasionally pointing at the car, and its sort-of famous driver, had been taken away. Not only was it a badge of honour, but also a good way of gaining some minor celebrity in your local neighbourhood, and now the bloody taxman had spoiled their fun. I know players who have asked the garage to sticker up their car with their name, even though they weren't actually sponsored by them.

What you ended up driving during the season was sometimes down to pot luck, but it could also depend on how well the team did the previous year. When we had a good year, the commercial manager did a sponsorship with the local BMW dealership so we drove around in top-of-the-range saloons all summer. When things weren't so good in other years we might end up with a mid-range Skoda or a Nissan for the season and, as happened to me once, have to spend six hours driving to Old Trafford on a traffic-choked M6 with the least talkative of your team-mates and no radio to entertain you because the bloke at the Skoda garage didn't know the key code.

Every now and then you and a team-mate would have to drive the kit van to away games, which was great fun and used to be a good way of losing some weight. None of these things used to have air-conditioning so you could easily shed a few pounds doing a long stint to Glamorgan with the outside temperature gauge nudging into the 30s and you, topless and sweating your arse off, living your best trucker's life. Imagine telling Harry Kane and Gareth Bale they had to drive to Spurs' kit to a game at Newcastle. You would sit there stewing on the M6 sometimes wondering whether this really was the best preparation for a professional athlete.

I remember turning up at Old Trafford to train before a game the next day and only about half of the lads had made it. Two of my team-mates had just taken delivery of new Mercs but filled them up with the wrong fuel and were sitting on the M1 waiting to be towed to the garage.

Players like to get from game A to game B as quickly as they can, which can lead to all sorts of problems about things like parking tickets and speeding fines. It can cause ructions in a team when players argue over who was driving when the speed camera flashed, or who parked on a yellow line outside the hotel and got a parking ticket because the driver couldn't be arsed to use the off-site hotel car park a couple of hundred yards down the road. I remember once a car sponsor coming into the club office after the season finished with a huge wad of parking tickets he had found in the glove compartments of his vehicles. The club invariably end up paying all the fines.

Certain players refused to travel with team-mates because their driving was so bad. A mate of mine at another county wouldn't get in the car because his companion would be doing 100mph as soon as he got on the motorway. Quite often I would make up a story about speed cameras to stop a team-mate going too fast. It's the same in any walk of life. Some people drive fast and you feel safe. Others don't. Cricketers tend to fall into the second category. We always seem to be in a hurry.

Of course, cars need fuel before they can get anywhere and this presents another problem – tightwads who refuse to pay for petrol because they can't be bothered to fill in an expenses form and claim it back from the club. I remember when I started and was earning £8k a year having to fill up the tank because my regular passenger, who was earning £100k, refused to pay for £50 worth of petrol. One favourite scam used to be when a player drives his own car, bungs 100 extra miles on the expense claim (no one ever checked in the accounts department) and claims another £40 from the club on expenses.

A bit of advice for players coming into the game – always keep your receipts. Not only can you claim it back (in the old days expenses used to be paid out in cash) from the club but it helps in disputes over speeding fines. I remember going down the motorway with a couple of team-mates following a game at Edgbaston and we got flashed just outside Birmingham. I wasn't driving, because it was my turn to take over after I had put petrol in at the last services. My team-mate was convinced I'd been speeding until I produced the petrol receipt and he ended up with three points, which I took great delight in pointing out to him was more than the number of runs he'd scored in the game.

I'm amazed and extremely thankful that cricketers haven't been killed or seriously injured driving from one venue to another during the past few years. Most players have had scrapes or been involved in near misses caused when they have fallen asleep at the wheel and woken just in time to stop the car careering towards the central reservation. I remember coming back from a T20 game at the end of a heavy playing schedule a few years ago with two team-mates and we swapped the driving every 20 minutes because we were all so knackered, and that was for a 90-minute journey.

I think any trip over two hours or so should be done by coach and that method of travel has become pretty much the norm in the past few years. A lot of counties get to use the same coaches as Premier League football clubs which have nice seating, lots of legroom, toilets, Sky TV, Wi-Fi and even kitchens. When you're one on of those and someone else is driving, life is good. But I have also been on a very long journey on what was effectively a school bus, which pulled over on to the hard shoulder a couple of times so everyone could have a piss in the lay-by because there was no toilet.

Wherever I lay my head …

What constitutes a good hotel for cricketers? I've stayed in so many that I like to think I am a bit of an expert. My criteria would be somewhere that is close to the ground or, if you're travelling by coach, a place with a nice bar that's in the middle of town. Of course, what constitutes a good hotel for club accountants or even sports scientists and physios is a different matter entirely.

The White House in Worcester was consistently the worst place I have stayed in. For many years it had no air-conditioning (or, if it did, it never worked when I stayed), and for some reason, even though Worcester is miles from the nearest coastline, it seemed to attract a hefty seagull population to its roof and windows. Result, next to no sleep for five nights. When we knew we were staying there again one year, I tried to book into the Premier Inn on the ground at New Road at my own expense, but couldn't get in. 'How the hell did it come to this?' I thought. 'I am a well-paid professional sportsman and the hotel we are in is so shit I am willing to pay for myself to stay in a Premier Inn.' Fuck my life … sometimes.

I just wished the clubs would consult the players a bit more when they book hotels. This job is normally done in the middle of winter and it's amazing how a bit of clever photography on a website can persuade the club secretary or accountant that a certain hotel looks fine and, more importantly, is well within budget. In a lot of places the reality is somewhat different. The gym is the same size as one of the rooms and the swimming pool is full once the team have all got in for the end-of-day lay cool-down session. Bookings rarely seem to be made by someone who has the slightest idea about the specific needs of professional athletes.

Over the years I have lost count of the number of team-mates who have kipped on my floor because their room was next to the motorway or a busy road and too noisy. Once, a team-mate, an England player incidentally, dragged his mattress to my room and slept there for three nights, convinced his room was haunted because the door that opened up on to a dividing wall kept rattling.

Cricket teams don't stay in budget hotels because they don't tend to have gyms or swimming pools, which most clubs insist on now for recovery sessions after a day's play. The wealthier Test-match counties tend to let all their players have some privacy and their own room. But doing that can double the cost of an away trip so you can see why smaller counties still make players share. But professional cricketers need their sleep.

Some players have it written in their contract that they get their own room and it's a privilege normally given to the captain and coach. But a lot of the time we are still sharing, which can be fun if you have a regular partner who keeps reasonable hours, doesn't hog the bathroom in the morning and doesn't snore.

However, if you end up with someone who does none of the above it can be a nightmare. Someone who snores or who stays up until the early hours watching porn on TV, phoning their girlfriend for hours on end or spending ages in the bathroom can make it a long few days. When I played second-team cricket at the start of my career, I would often be paired up with a triallist and for a young player the experience of sharing a bedroom with a complete stranger lying two feet away from you and talking in their sleep could be quite unnerving.

Once, after a few beers, one of my team-mates was sick all over the floor and a fair amount of that ended up on my duvet. Luckily, I slept through that and he paid the cleaning bill which was later sent to the club.

I have lost count of the number of times I have woken up to the sound of a team-mate pissing in the cupboard or against the table. Pissing in the wardrobe used to be a regular occurrence with one of my 'roomies'. I kept my clothes in my bag after the first time it happened when some of his 'spray' ended up on my Hugo Boss jeans.

The normal rule of etiquette is when one wants to go to sleep the other turns the volume down or tries to nod off. But sometimes he will insist on finishing the movie he's watching, only to fall asleep and you have to grope around under his covers making sure that it's the remote control you grab hold of.

One player came back from a winter playing abroad convinced he was now a yoga expert, and not just any old yoga expert. He liked to do it naked for two hours every night. My mate would sit there trying to watch TV or read his book while his spiritual friend would be chanting on the floor in the downward dog position.

The daily meal allowance when I started was £17.50 and all counties paid the same. In the subsequent 20 odd years it's gone up to … £18! Some players will stay in and save it, eating food they have taken from the ground which they will get heated up in a microwave at the hotel. Others are happy with

Subway or Nando's, but I have always liked to go out for a nice meal and a pint or a glass of wine during an away trip. Sometimes it can be the highlight of the week on the road, a bit like a holiday. I never stressed about how much it cost above my £18 allowance.

Men in white coats

In the same way that football has good referees and bad, so there are decent umpires and others who I wouldn't put in charge of a fifth XI match. But county cricket is not like the Premier League. There is no VAR, no recourse to instant replays. So when you think you're on the end of a poor decision the only way of checking is off the footage from the analysts' camera which is blowing in the breeze perched precariously on top of the sight screen. It's not a great guide as to whether the ball was outside the line or not.

I think what pisses players off most about umpires is that, unlike a player or coach, a bad umpire won't get the sack at the end of the season. It's been a bone of contention among players for many years. In my career I can only remember one umpire having to leave the first-class list for consistently poor performances, and there were other factors in that decision as well.

Generally speaking, it's a pretty easy job. You can go on until you're 65 or even beyond and you're on £50–70k a year with all expenses paid for six months' work, so it's a nice lifestyle. I know coaches mark the performance of umpires at the end of every game, but the bad ones still seem to stay in a job. Coaches will take feedback from players when they rate the umpire, but if he thinks the umpire has had a good game, even if you've been on the end of an awful decision, it's unlikely in my experience to sway his judgement.

In the same way players play shit shots, umpires make bad decisions, but good ones have the grace to admit it. You have a lot more respect for someone who has given you out but then has a look at the replay, realised he's had a shocker and apologised, like a few have done to me over the years. My estimation of the umpire who can take it on the chin and admit their fallibility goes up immediately.

With the technology available now, there should be a system whereby a player can provide constructive criticism anonymously that gets fed back to the umpire. I would say umpires earn more money than probably 50% of county pros, but sometimes I don't think they do enough to earn it. It's no wonder the waiting list for an umpires' job is growing.

You normally know when you find out who is umpiring your game, particularly if it's in the County Championship, whether it's going to be all over in three days and you get an unscheduled day off (unless you lose of course, in which case you'll invariably be called in for net practice).

I remember standing at the non-striker's end during the opening overs of a game chatting to the umpire. 'I've been on the road for 25 days, I'm absolutely shattered,' he told me. The next time I spoke to my batting partner at the end of the over I told him that this game would not go into a fourth day. There were 24 lbws, of which he gave 17, and the game barely made it to lunch on the third day. He triggered me twice, the second time when the ball wouldn't have hit another set. I saw him as he was leaving the ground. 'Enjoy your day off!' Hopefully, he detected the sarcastic, rather bitter tone in my voice.

If you bat between 40 and 50 times a season I reckon you'll be on the end of between 10 and 15 very debatable decisions. In a good season, if I'd scored a lot of runs, most would have gone my way. Sometimes the difference between a good or bad season can be a single dodgy umpiring decision. I remember a game early in the season on an absolute road where I got a shocking lbw on the first morning. I had to watch the rest of the team churn out 650 and the umpire just laughed when I tried to show him the replay. After a few beers at the end of the season, I reminded him it cost me £5k when I ended up eight runs short of a bonus.

But it works both ways. I have had seasons when it has gone my way, the early lbw I got when I was bowling and ended up with five wickets, and the times when I got the benefit of the doubt and went on to make a big score. With the schedule we play, I think umpires generally err on the side of the bowler to keep the game moving. In which case, why didn't I cultivate relationships with umpires so I would get the benefit of the doubt more often? That happens, but sometimes you'll get on well with an umpire and he gives you a stinking decision and you wonder why you bothered!

Some umpires can fold under pressure. The players all know who the 'weak' ones are. I always knew in front of certain umpires that my chances of being out if I was hit on the pad increased because they struggled when the opposition put them under pressure with incessant appealing.

There would always be certain fixtures when you would see the umpires on duty and wonder how the fuck they would cope with the egos of some of the players. The big teams who can put pressure on the weaker umpires knew it and it would be an uphill battle.

But then at the other end of the scale you had guys like Peter Willey, who was a great umpire and a really nice bloke. If you pissed him off, he would show you what he thought of you which may sound crap but it meant you built a good relationship with him.

The best umpires pull you up gently. 'Pipe down' and 'chill out' seem to be the favourite expressions of a lot of umpires. If he notices the ball looks a bit dodgy, a good umpire will have a quiet word with the captain and warn them. They communicate all the time, treat the players like adults and if a team transgresses guys like Michael Gough and Richard Kettleborough, for instance, will come down hard on them.

Gough, Kettleborough, Alex Wharf and Ian Gould are all brilliant. I would call them professional umpires. Gunner Gould umpires in a great way and mostly gets the decisions right. He would abuse players, too, but in a nice way. I remember him getting really pissed off with Mark Cosgrove, the Australian batsman who played for Leicestershire when he was behaving like a dickhead. He kept querying his decisions, so Gunner told him exactly what he thought of his body shape which we all found amusing, including Cosgrove.

On one occasion I got some great advice from Nick Cook, who had played for England and played as well as I ever did. These guys watch a lot of cricket so they generally know their stuff and can be great sources of tips and advice. I've always wondered why England selectors didn't consult them more. They have the best view of the players, seven days a week, and can spot a good player.

Good umpires take their time over decisions; they're composed, they don't overreact and they're not trying to make friends. Incidentally, Kettleborough is referred to by the journalists on the county circuit as Umpire Who Boasts. Apparently, when he was playing for Yorkshire years ago, a reporter was overheard in the Headingley press box dictating copy to his newspaper office and came up with 'Richard

Kettleborough, comma, who boasts the longest surname in first-class cricket, comma' ... brilliant.

In recent years quite a few more former players have gone into umpiring to stay connected to the game, but I wouldn't say it has made a big difference to the overall standard. You can normally tell quite quickly if they are any good. I remember playing in a game where Alex Wharf was standing with a guy with 15 years' more experience and you'd have thought Wharf was the senior man.

Maybe more technology would help. VAR in football is a contentious subject, but it has helped reduce the number of bad decisions by referees and their assistants. Maybe one day in county cricket a version of the DRS will be introduced to help umpires, but also put them under a bit more scrutiny than they are at the moment. The technology is there, but it's a costly business and employing it at Derbyshire v Northants in front of 300 people at a freezing-cold ground in April might not be the best use of the ECB's resources.

WAGs

The term WAGs (wives and girlfriends) came from football, and it may surprise you to know that there is a WAGs culture in county cricket. Well, sort of.

To be fair to counties they have upped their game with how they look after players' families during matches. Invariably the families will come along to a T20 on a Friday night when it is blowing a gale and fairly unpleasant. Thankfully, clubs now appreciate that a few plastic chairs and a bottle of lukewarm Lambrini isn't sufficient to keep the long-suffering families happy during a game. Most clubs will have a hospitality box set aside for everyone, but it can be a tough call for the commercial manager to forego £10k for a big game to give access to it to the families.

The warm summer evenings when everyone sits outside as the sun goes down with a bottle of rosé are few and far between, so it is important that as players we can see our families are warm and comfortable. But on occasion I have looked over and seen my family sitting on plastic chairs next to a particularly rowdy stand and been genuinely worried for them if the pissheads found out public enemy No.1's family was sitting ten yards away, separated by a bit of rope and a pensioner in a fluorescent jacket doing stewarding duties.

Our wives and girlfriends go through a hell of a lot while we are out on the field chasing our dreams. Endless weeks and winters spent on their own as we tour places like the West Indies or Australia are a hefty price to pay when we come home in a foul mood after a shit day. A lot of relationships fall apart along the way because both parties struggle to deal with the time they spend apart and the fact that the cricket calendar will determine when and how long we get to spend together.

The county cricket community

We're pretty lucky as cricketers compared to other sportsmen. If we get out for a duck or get hit for four successive boundaries there might be a few tut-tuts in the crowd, but all that most county cricket supporters want is you and the team to do well. Getting a standing ovation as you walk off a ground after making a big contribution towards a victory is a fantastic feeling.

Most supporters of county teams are genuinely lovely people. Some will follow their county all over the country and it's nice to see a few familiar faces dotted around the boundary when you turn up for an away match miles from home. They will invariably contribute towards a player's benefit or testimonial fund even if they haven't got much spare cash themselves. They love their team and they love cricket. You can grow quite close to them, it's a relationship which I think is unique to cricket.

I know that county cricket attracts its fair share of oddballs and eccentrics, but I think it's all part of the charm of the game. I would certainly never criticise them because without those people, who take all their holiday from work so they can watch cricket or retirees who probably make up three-quarters of the crowd at a Championship game, there would be no one watching, and we all need an audience.

It's like a little community all of its own. For less than a couple of hundred quid you can watch professional sport for six months of the year, quite often in nice weather, along with your friends. I know for a lot of people that the sense of community it offers – the chance to chat to people with a shared passion – can sometimes be the only social interaction they might get on a regular basis. There's something quite comforting about that. When I give up work, I'll probably end up sitting alongside them, helping to form that wall of BO for the players to walk through. They should really give out County Championship memberships as part of the state pension, it would give elderly people a ready-made community to be part of even if they didn't like cricket.

The wider world

You won't be surprised that in most county dressing-rooms we talk about the same stuff you do in an office or a factory: football, *Love Island*, celebrities, the usual stuff. A lot of players have the benefit of private education, supposed to make them more rounded individuals when they enter the wider world. But in reality a cricket team are no different to the rest of society. Outside the game we're all interested in the same stuff and how events will affect us.

I have played with some intelligent guys who have fascinating views. One of my old team-mates was an archetypal old-school opening bowler, brought up in club cricket and educated at his local comprehensive, but he was an engaging conversationalist on a whole range of subjects, including politics, and held some interesting opinions.

There is a perception because of the background of most of them that county cricketers tend to be right-wing in their political views. I'm not so sure this is the case now, especially since the Brexit vote in 2016. I remember getting on the bus to go to an away game on the day of the 2015 general election and telling one of the lads who I had voted for. My other half works in the public sector and regularly tells me about the problems in our state systems. I have always been left-leaning. Anyway, this little nugget soon got around and I got some unbelievable stick from a few of the lads whose political views tended to be shaped by what they read on the front pages of the *Daily Mail* or *The Sun*.

I'm not particularly politically engaged, but I think it's always worth considering the wider picture when it's time to vote. Voting for one party may disadvantage me personally a bit, but if it will help a lot of other people I normally consider that worth it.

I love county cricket but …

If there was one regulation I could change in the Championship it would be ending games where there is no chance of a positive result at tea on the final day. I can't think of anything more futile in professional sport than the last-day post-tea session in a game that has long since been consigned to a draw. What amazes me is that people stay and give validity to it by watching as the opening batsman bowls loopy leg breaks or the wicketkeeper gives his pads to the opening bowler so he can turn his arm over and say that he once bowled to the England captain.

There is only one thing worse than being part of this farce and that's watching earnest young batsmen come in, make 60 or so runs to top up their average off what is effectively joke bowling, and then sit in the dressing-room afterwards and tell us that, actually, the opposition's opening batsman (career overs, 12) is a lot harder to face than he looks.

Another pet hate is declaration bowling. Fortunately, it's seldom employed these days but I remember making a hundred once in about ten overs and getting a standing ovation from the members. I could barely lift my bat to acknowledge them, such was my shame. Even the opposition slip fielders joined in, piss-taking gits. I did have some sympathy for my opening partner, though. The previous evening he'd got out for not many in the last over of the day. As we were walking off the opposition captain looked up at the scoreboard and told me they would set something up in the morning. As you can imagine, I couldn't wait to pass on this information to my partner ...

4

Feeling Like A Rock Star

I COUNT myself lucky compared to a lot of my contemporaries. I've played in Lord's finals, I've hit sixes at T20 Finals Day and I have had some nice pay days in franchise T20 competitions around the world. I've got no regrets about my career, but I sometimes wish I'd started, say, ten years later so I could have made the most of my talent and maximised my earning potential like some of the English players are doing now by increasingly concentrating on white-ball cricket.

One-day cricket has changed so much during my career and it will continue to evolve. In 20 years even something like The Hundred might seem old fashioned. Is there a day coming when we play 50-ball games or even shorter format matches than that? It wouldn't surprise me, although the T10 debacle at the start of 2021 and the scintillating Test cricket being played in Australia and India at the same time makes me think there is still a future for longer forms of the game. The lack of skill and identity in the T10 format may not make it a long-term fix commercially.

Nothing has dominated conversations in county dressing-rooms in the past couple of years more than The Hundred and the majority of county pros, and certainly all those lucky enough to get a contract, want it to succeed. We all care passionately that the game increases its appeal to a wider audience because it has a direct effect on our livelihoods.

But I also think we can do things better to improve the product and provide the entertainment that the vast majority of cricket fans, new and old, want to see. For me, that means doing away with the domestic 50-over competition and making T20 a quicker game to play and watch. So here are some thoughts on one-day cricket and what it needs to do to keep existing fans interested and attract new ones when competition for your average person's money and attention has never been greater.

The best of times

Standing in front of that jam-packed OCS Stand at the Oval or the heaving Hollies Stand at Edgbaston on Finals Day is the nearest thing I ever got to the adulation a Premier League footballer or the headline act at Glastonbury will enjoy. It's unbelievable.

I remember taking a catch at the Oval once. It probably wasn't among the top ten in my career, but I had to sprint 50 yards and dive to hold on. The sort I'd back myself to take eight times out of ten. When I came up with the ball the crowd were going nuts. I bowed in front of them and they lapped it up. It wasn't quite like the one Ben Stokes held in roughly the same place during the 2019 World Cup game against South Africa, but not far off. It's something I will never forget.

I have been lucky enough to play at Finals Day and in front of packed houses around the world. I would really struggle to pick a favourite experience. Playing on the subcontinent is a different world in terms of noise and colour, but Finals Day is amazing, the crowd are great fun, and it is such a huge occasion. Lord's is a special place to play with a full house and I have been so fortunate to enjoy so many special memories, whether we won or lost.

Finals Day is a totally unique experience. Each of the four counties will have a few hundred of their fans tucked away, but the vast majority are neutrals, there for sixes, the mascot race, beer snakes and a day-long piss-up. But winning there is very special and when you get the chance to absorb the atmosphere and take in the sights and sounds, you know that it's not going to get much better for a county cricketer.

I'd say on average that three-quarters of the crowd at a T20 don't really care too much who wins. Most will have forgotten the result by the time they get home. I have played in front of 25,000 at the Oval and apart from a couple of hundred members in the pavilion, I don't think many of the fans even knew who Surrey were playing. All the vast majority want to see is the ball disappear into the crowd a couple of times an over and the orange stumps splattered now and again. They are not asking for much really. I'd be the same if I were watching. But if I smash a six into the crowd and a youngster catches the ball in front of their parents and appears on the big screen it's created a memory that can help get he or she hooked on the game.

You don't quite feel like a rock star when you play a T20 at Lord's; in fact it's a bit like playing on the big lawn in front of Downton Abbey at a garden party. I know most the crowd, like The Oval, is also made up of City-types on a night out, but the atmosphere is completely different. Even the opposition get applauded for good play.

At the other end of the scale there is Chelmsford. Now that is a ground where it does feel like you are stepping on enemy territory. There used to be a spot near to the pavilion that was very lively. I've seen a couple of fights with punches and plastic containers of lager sent flying. It's like a football crowd, but a crowd you might have found on the terraces at Upton Park in the 1980s.

One year I turned up for a Friday night game there and discovered that this infamous spot by the pavilion had been turned into a Family Stand and by the time we started it was full of families and kids.

Clever marketing by Essex, I thought. They are trying to gentrify the place a bit. A couple of overs in I went to field the ball in front of the stand and it bobbled horribly – which happens a lot at Chelmsford in the height of summer when the outfield gets bone-dry.

It rolled to the rope, there was plenty of ironic cheering as I'd expected and as I went to pick it up a kid who can't have been more than seven or eight peered over the ad board. 'You're a useless c**t!' I looked up and his dad stood up behind him. 'You tell him son, he is a useless c**t and he knows it!' It remains the only time I was called the c-word on a county ground by someone other than an opponent (and the occasional team-mate).

Reinventing yourself

There are a few still kicking around in county cricket; guys who hardly play one-day cricket but in ten years, perhaps even sooner, I don't think there will be any on county staffs. Their value to their club is diminishing all the time and I can even see a situation where they are more likely to play as amateurs thn fully-fledged professionals in the Championship, a bit like it had been in our game for two-thirds of the 20th century.

Within the next ten years I reckon 30–40% of our professionals will only play white-ball stuff. As a big fan of the County Championship that is hard for me to contemplate, but it's the reality. Anyone who just plays Championship matches and isn't good enough to play Test cricket will earn about £40k a year tops. Decent money, but not a salary you are going to be able to retire on. Most of the best bonuses and incentives these days go on the contracts of players who play white-ball cricket and are good at it.

They will do all the training in winter and pre-season, start the summer and then when the T20 or 50-over competition starts, they either kick their heels or go and play in the second team. Believe me, the only thing worse than watching your team-mates play T20 cricket in front of a packed house on a Friday night is having to go and play the same game in the seconds at a club ground in front of 20 people, but that happens all the time to the red-ball specialists. A lot of them struggle to deal with it.

I have spoken to a few team-mates who I could see were getting pigeonholed in this way and warned them they had no future if they didn't play white-ball cricket. These days, being able to play a classic forward defensive to a 90mph bowler is not much use to your career if you can't hit 20 off five balls at the tail end of a T20 innings, or defend ten runs off the last over when you're shitting yourself because it will be down to you if you lose.

But can players like that reinvent themselves and be white-ball guns? Absolutely. Players who specialise in red-ball cricket tend to be very good technically. A white-ball player might have less pure talent, but if they are good at the basics, keep themselves supremely fit and can adapt quickly to different countries and conditions they have the basics for a very lucrative career.

If you are a good red-ball cricketer you should have the fundamentals to be able to adapt your game. If you can play a forward defensive, you should be able to hit a six. If you can bowl a yorker, or well-disguised slower ball, you ought to be able to bowl another in the same over. I think a lot of it is a mental shift, changing the way you practise, and getting coaches on board as you alter the habits of a lifetime. You can get stronger in the gym to enable you to hit the ball further or bowl it quicker. You can improve your sharpness over shorter distances. There are so many ways you can improve yourself mentally that will enable you to make decisions in a split-second with more clarity.

I think it's harder to do it the other way around, but then again a white-ball specialist is unlikely to suddenly decide he wants to be a Test player in this day and age. Certainly not for financial reasons, anyway.

Things are changing and counties are placing more emphasis on white-ball cricket than they did even five years ago. Yet it's still the case that most players on a county staff spend 80% of their time in practice, especially during pre-season, working with a red ball when their main value to their club has to be the ability to bowl four tight overs regularly, or have a strike rate between 140 and 160 with the bat.

Look at someone like Somerset's Tom Banton, who probably spends 10% of his practice time with a red ball. He's a brilliant one-day player, he is in the England set-up now and he's got contracts in the IPL and Big Bash. Good luck to him. Why would he want to try and get in the England Test team when he can earn the thick end of half a million pounds a year playing white-ball cricket, comfortable in the knowledge that, if he stays fit and healthy, he can keep doing it for the best part of ten years and set himself up for life? What if he shifted to 80% red-ball practice in the winter and turned up to play at the start of the season on a couple of green tops where he doesn't stand a chance? He already has a three- or four-year window to cash in on the past two years of eye-catching performances – why risk that to play the moving ball in April for the possibility of playing Test cricket?

Other players who I think have their heads screwed on are Sussex's Phil Salt and Lancashire's Liam Livingstone, who only know one way to play. These guys are typical franchise guns for hire, playing all over the world and maximising their earning power. Even if they don't play for England much – and I think they probably will – they will still have a rewarding career, both in cricketing terms and financially. And if they have to make a choice between going off to play T20 somewhere for three weeks and earning £80k, or facing the new ball at Derby on a bleak April morning, what do you think they will do? Don't say Derby, I know you love county cricket, but it's the wrong answer and you know it.

At the end of the day, playing cricket is a job and players must decide the best way of optimising their earning power. I admire guys like Stokes and Jofra Archer who are driven to be the best they can in all formats, and who are rewarded accordingly. But I am pretty certain they belong to the last generation of players who will think that way.

For the first two-thirds of my career, I thought the same as Stokes and Archer. But for the past five years or so, I was in the Banton, Salt or Eoin Morgan camp because I recognised that the only way I could prolong my career was to put more emphasis on white-ball cricket. County cricketers in England are increasingly starting to think the same, but it remains a gradual process.

Since T20 started in England in 2003 it has grown to become a brilliant competition, but other countries cottoned on and created their own versions which became bigger and better. As the Indian Premier League and Big Bash took hold, and then a myriad of smaller tournaments started up, I adjusted my own practice time accordingly and split it 70–30 in favour of improving my white-ball skills. I couldn't break into the top echelons and earn myself a contract at the IPL or Big Bash unfortunately, but I did play in other competitions around the world.

These days, if your record stands up and you have a well-connected agent you can pick up opportunities to play franchise cricket abroad for ten months of the year and earn a nice pay packet. Not life-changing sums, but £3k a game and all expenses paid in a ten-game tournament for three weeks is decent money.

Fitter, faster, stronger

As T20 took off, I realised I needed to be fitter, that I had to learn new shots, find out which deliveries gave me a better chance of getting wickets, and what my stock ball was. I knew I had to be more agile in the field, to be able to throw the ball further and with more accuracy and to stay mentally alert so I could think straight when the pressure was on, which happens quite often during a T20 game.

The game was constantly evolving, and if you didn't keep up you were left behind, especially when you got older and suddenly younger, fitter and perhaps technically better versions of yourself came on to the staff looking to take your slot. No sooner than you thought you'd nailed the sweep, someone like Kevin Pietersen started reverse-hitting the ball into the stands. Of course, people hit sixes in the early years of T20, but you never saw anyone rocking on to the back foot and hitting a back-of-a-length ball from a spinner over wide long-on like, say, Glenn Maxwell does. The last few years for all white-ball players has been a constant process of re-evaluation and re-invention.

Even right up until the past couple of years I was still trying to improve. As an example, it wasn't until the last few years of my career that I learnt how to properly sweep quicker bowlers, a shot no one had played for the majority of my career, but which had now become de rigueur.

I would pick up tips just by watching other players in games, on TV or if the analyst spotted something. You would go into the nets and try things out for yourself. And once you felt you had perfected it, you needed to have the strength of mind to recognise that this was another opportunity for you to score runs, even if you got out playing it two or three times in a row while you perfected the shot in a match situation.

Sweeping was my weakest shot, but fortunately because I was so strong in other areas, I didn't really need to play it much. As I played more, and the game evolved, it was expected that you would be able to play all sorts of sweeps. You used to get a bollocking if you got out playing one, now it's no different to a forward defensive.

For maybe a decade after T20 started in 2003, a lot of the shots which you see all the time had to be learnt, or at least worked on to a much greater extent by the majority of English players. Now, every player can ramp, reverse sweep quicker bowlers and spinners, slog sweep and power hit. That is part of the role, the basics really. Fifteen years or so ago, if you could bowl a good yorker you were pretty sure it wouldn't go for six. Now, they can disappear as easily as a wide half-volley outside off stump.

My advice to any aspiring T20 batsman is to get as high as you can in the order as quickly as you can.

In England, you might come across the odd really quick bowler who also gets bounce, but there is still a predominance of right-armers who move it away and left-armers who swing it back at around 80–85mph. Hitting that should be a piece of piss. Just free your arms and help yourself.

There will always be room for bowlers who might lack out-and-out pace, but make up for it with their ability to deliver their skill consistently under pressure, someone like Benny Howell at Gloucestershire, who is consistently improvising and improving. You can't afford to stand still. Look at Worcestershire's Pat

Brown. He was a massive part of their success in 2019, but he went from taking 48 T20 wickets in two seasons, earning England recognition and a gig in The Hundred, to eight wickets in eight games in 2020. Batsmen had worked him out.

Will someone like him evolve and reach the top again? I hope so, because he has a lot of great skills, but this is the challenge facing T20 players with bat and ball and highlights why it is so hard to be a top performer year in year out. It is these guys I have the most respect for, as it doesn't just happen. The best players are constantly working hard to improve and adapt as the opposition works them out. Give me a player who has strung eight good seasons together over a youngster who scored a flashy fifty on TV any day. Players need bottle, that is what wins you trophies and makes long and successful careers.

Be lucky

Every player needs a bit of good fortune and even more so in T20 because the margins between success and failure are tiny. But it's also a lot easier to get back into nick than it is against the red ball, sometimes it only needs a couple of deliveries.

These days in every game you will see at least one outstanding piece of fielding. Those clips that go viral on social media, when a fielder hares around the outfield, steps across the boundary cushion and parries the ball back on to the field before completing the catch have almost become the norm. Great for the fielder, not so for the batsman who thinks he's nailed it for six and ends up standing there saying, 'Did he just do that?' If it happens again in the next game, and the one after, and suddenly you've got ten runs in three games and your place is under threat, then you will need the strength of character to keep believing in your ability to consistently deliver your skills.

When you're out of nick there is never any point in spending a long time in the nets trying to rectify it, unless an obvious technical flaw that needs fixing has crept into your game. The key is to do the work before the season or tournament, put the hours in and once the competition is going it is about topping up and being in the right frame of mind day after day. It is bloody hard being underprepared before a tournament and then chasing your tail after five games. All you can do is move on to the next innings and accept that luck might go your way next time. You go out, inside edge your first ball for four then hit the next over midwicket for six because the boundary is tiny and there's a strong breeze at your back when on another day it would be an easy catch. Suddenly, you have ten runs off two deliveries and you're flying. When it is like that, just ride the wave. You can be in and out of form in two balls.

I have played in games where things have all gone my way. I may have prepared and played exactly the same, but in one game the first ball I hit went straight through a fielder's hands for four, the next the same fielder dived full length and caught it one-handed. I have had stinking tournaments where every ball I hit was stopped or caught, and others where I just could not get out. I have bowled exactly where I wanted and gone for 20 an over and bowled an absolute shower of shit and got five-for.

T20 is that kind of game and the best players and coaches see through the numbers and get that. Coaches in T20 didn't realise this at first, but this generation of coaches have played the game and understand how it works.

When it's going well it is the best feeling. The crowd love it, your average is going through the roof and the coach wants to talk about extending your contract – you walk out to bat and don't think you're going to get out. Lovely. Full houses and TV games mean you get a bit more of a celebrity profile and more followers on social media. You also start to think about the deals coming your way and the cash that comes with them.

Don't look at the averages

Averages in T20 cricket are a waste of time. I don't pay much attention to them, even mine, because so many factors are at play.

For instance, it can make a hell of a difference to your figures if you're playing half of your games at Taunton or Trent Bridge, where 200 is a par score, or if you get to bowl overs 7, 9, 11 and 13 with the breeze behind you at certain grounds.

I remember a team-mate going into contract discussions and being told his T20 average was too low to warrant a pay rise. The guy batted at No.7 and averaged less than ten balls faced over two seasons. How's he meant to average 30? The only columns that need concern you are economy rates for bowlers and strike rates for batsmen.

Hedging your bets

I was fortunate. The counties I played for wanted to win the Championship and one-day competitions, or certainly be competitive across the different formats, but I don't think there is anything wrong with those clubs who in recent years have tended to concentrate on T20 and 50-over cricket and populated their squads accordingly.

Let's face it, 60% of counties are probably never going to win the Championship, so what is the problem with shifting your priorities? Shorter formats are much more of a level playing field and if you get your recruitment right, as Northamptonshire and Leicestershire have done in recent years, you can bloody the noses of the bigger counties, even with a much smaller playing budget and fewer high-quality players.

After all, these are the competitions where clubs sell more tickets, more hospitality and more replica shirts. It makes perfect sense to exploit the market, although I still believe that, for now at least, most English players still want to be part of a competitive red-ball side.

But you can see why some of us pros are happy to go and play for the so-called smaller counties, knowing that the emphasis is on one-day cricket, especially if a lighter workload prolongs their careers for four or five years and they can earn decent money.

It's down to the individual's ego in the end. I couldn't have done it. I would have needed a lot of money to commit to five years playing for a small county, but that's me. I felt I was good enough to play for big clubs at big grounds and I wanted to do that for as long as possible, competing for trophies rather than focusing on a white-ball competition.

On the surface

One of the best developments in one-day cricket in the last couple of years is the wider use of hybrid pitches. In fact, I can't think of anything else which could so fundamentally improve the skill level in our domestic one-day competitions and particularly T20.

It's great to think that in future years the vast majority of T20 and even 50-over games might be played on decent surfaces that offer a hybrid mixture of normal and artificial grass. In my experience, even those used three or four times still provide good pace and carry, and they turn a bit as well.

I think counties should be instructed that their three central pitches, which are the ones used for games shown on TV, must be hybrid. You ought to be able to play most of your group-stage games on one of them. And because they are centrally positioned it means bowlers are less disadvantaged than they often find themselves when they are playing further along the square when even average batsmen can bunt mishits over the short boundary for six. Bowlers hate that.

Any technological development that stops us playing on slow shit-heaps that have been played on three or four times already has to be welcomed. No one more than the players themselves recognise that T20 is all about entertaining people, but I have lost count of the number of games I was involved in at the back end of the group stage of the Blast when 120/8 played 115/7 and a six was as rare as hen's teeth.

You would field on the boundary in these games and all you could hear people in the crowd talking about was everything except what was going on in front of them. Believe me, if you have watched such a game I can tell you that they are as boring to play in as they are to watch. There is a reason why people get handed 6 and 4 cards to wave in the air and not ones with a dot or lbw on them.

Of course, counties want to make the most of home advantage, but isn't playing half of your games in familiar surroundings enough? My heart sank when we turned up at Lancashire to discover that the game we were about to play was on a pitch that has already been used five times, as I did a few years ago. It takes the piss out of the players and takes people paying good money for granted.

Is it any coincidence that the counties who play on poor pitches tend to get small crowds? Sophia Gardens in Cardiff is the best example – predominantly low-scoring games on a ground where it's harder to hit sixes anyway because the square boundaries are quite long, played in front of 3,000 people dotted around a 15,000-capacity stadium. It's amazing to think that Finals Day was held there one year. Thankfully, it returned to its rightful home at Edgbaston the following season, where the atmosphere is always as it should be.

Bring back the Pro40

Forty overs or 50? For me this is a no-brainer. Why we jettisoned the 40 overs competition a few years ago still baffles me. If the ECB polled the players and supporters, I am convinced they would back 40 overs instead of 50.

We were told that we were reverting to 50 overs because it mirrored international competition, but I don't think that argument carries any weight these days. The one-day game has moved on so much in the past few years.

Did playing it again really pave the way for our World Cup success in 2019? I would argue not. For starters, most of the senior guys in that squad learnt about white-ball cricket from playing a mixture of 20 and 40 overs stuff at the start of their careers or, in the case of the younger players, predominantly T20. The 40-over competition was brilliant, players loved it. Afternoon starts, finishes under floodlights and far bigger crowds than those we play in front of for 50-over games. And it's also an opportunity to improve skills you can easily transfer into T20. I'd bring it back in a heartbeat and let the players enjoy an occasional lie-in. Losing 20 overs definitely helped with the issue of fatigue and injuries. Crowds were great and the quality of cricket was always high.

Sort out the schedule

In recent years, the ECB have made more of an effort to make the fixture list more coherent, but even in 2020, when the domestic schedule was curtailed by Covid-19, the shortened T20 qualifying competition still contained a random four-day game in the middle.

Memo to ECB fixtures department: as soon as the schedule is released the first thing players look for are: their first game; their longest run of continuous days playing; when their longest trip is; and if there's a four-dayer in the middle of the T20.

They can't do much about the first two, but surely it's possible to play all our T20 games in a block? We're not even fussed when that is, although it makes sense to play the tournament in the height of summer and when kids are on holiday from school.

But no. A typical week can start on a Saturday with travel and training followed by a four-day game from Sunday to Wednesday. You travel back, do T20 training on Thursday and then play on Friday, traditionally the best day for crowds at most counties. It's the one night of the week when we ought to be at our best so we can produce good entertainment. Instead, by that stage, most of us are knackered.

After an adrenaline-fuelled T20 game, the comedown can take hours. You might go to bed at 1am, fall asleep at 2.30 and then get up the next morning at 7 to start a Championship match four hours later – or you have been on a coach travelling half the night to get to a distant away ground. It's like deciding halfway through the French Open that they are going to play two rounds of doubles on a grass court.

The Hundred

During 2018 the thing we spoke about in the dressing-room more than anything – to the detriment of almost everything else if I'm honest – was The Hundred, the ECB's new competition designed to get cricket to a wider and more diverse audience.

We spoke about whether we needed another competition; what effect it would have on our other domestic tournaments, especially the T20 Blast; and, more than anything else, our chances of getting picked up in the auction and trousering £35k minimum for a month's work.

We also had a good laugh along the way, mostly about some of the hapless marketing initiatives that seemed to follow one after another with depressing regularity. The one where the ECB was pilloried after they used a picture of a rap concert in America to represent the audience they were seeking was my particular favourite.

I am not opposed to The Hundred, although I don't think I'm alone in finding some of the marketing concepts a bit odd. The disjointed announcements, the mixed messaging as to why the competition is needed and what I thought were patronising comments about whether members of the target audience understood the concept of six-ball overs all contributed to the confusion. Not to mention the huge amount of money spent to create it. It felt a bit like the moment Allen Stanford's helicopter landed at Lord's with a plastic box containing one million dollars.

For me, The Hundred is a risk we don't need to be taking. A better strategy would have been to invest in the Blast and make sure that product is the very best it can be. If the competition's profile hasn't grown by 2025 by all means try something else.

If The Hundred brings a new audience to cricket, then great. And ticket sales were good, even before the pandemic struck in 2020 and the launch had to be put back 12 months. Everyone wants to see grounds packed and fans watching the best players in the world. The opportunity for English players to train, play and learn from some of the game's elite can only improve their game as well.

But some things disappointed me. I think it's an own goal not to have more home-grown coaches in the tournament. What an opportunity for up-and-coming coaches such as Vikram Solanki or Richard Dawson to head up a team full of international players. I know plenty have got jobs as assistants, but how much more benefit would it be for our coaches to have the opportunities in senior decision-making roles, working with some of the best players in the world. It's a small thing, and it might not be relevant to the paying public, but I think it is a missed opportunity by the ECB.

I accept that a few of the head coaches have been chosen because of their links to the grounds where their team is based, like Stephen Fleming, who used to play for Nottinghamshire, at Trent Rockets and Darren Lehmann, formerly of Yorkshire, with Northern Superchargers, who will play at Headingley. The auction raised some eyebrows on the circuit. Find me a player in county cricket who didn't spit their green tea out on at least five occasions when someone we had barely heard of suddenly got picked up for £50k while some of the biggest names were sitting at home oiling their bat in anticipation of a payday, only to discover they need not have bothered.

I have nothing against a fairly average cricketer getting paid way more than they should. Actually, screw that, I really do. The tournament was meant to be a reward for the top players. So how did we see someone who had less than ten games get picked ahead of players such as Dawid Malan or Luke Wright?

There are others who didn't get selected like Josh Cobb, Ian Cockbain and Rikki Wessels who must be bemused that they were overlooked in favour of others.

I will compare two players, and I won't name him, but I will call him Player A. He has one notable performance to his name, and that's about it. If you put him next to a Wright or a Malan he probably wouldn't be able to screw their spikes in, but at the auction Player A was selected about 40 picks before the world No.1 and England's highest T20 run scorer. This is where The Hundred lost a bit of credibility for me, and many others.

5

Country File

I DIDN'T play a lot of international cricket. So, if you are trying to work out who I am, there is one clue.

Mind you, there are quite a few of us in that category. For every Stokes, Archer and Root there are hundreds more players. Good, but not quite good enough to play at the highest level.

As I will explain, I knew pretty early in my career that the highest honours were going to elude me and with it the opportunity to earn life-changing sums of money.

I did play for the Lions, which I suppose is the next best thing, and I am proud of my England sweater and cap. I spent time in and around the England camp and enjoyed some great experiences with a bunch of outstanding players and offered me an unbelievable insight into what makes the very best players tick. I won't throw them away or flog them on eBay. Those few weeks did at least offer me a little insight into what it's like to play at the elite level.

I do know what it's like to face world-class opponents on a regular basis. I have played in front of massive crowds. And I have been around players who got picked for England and soon crashed and burned. Picking up the threads of their career and get back on the treadmill can be hard for them, and the rest of us dealing with the fallout.

Do I think there were players not as good as me who did play for England during my time? Yes, loads, and hundreds of other players will feel the same. But why does one player of similar age and comparable average get chosen ahead of someone else? Does it help what county you play for? Is there a window of time in your career when you think 'If I don't get picked now, I never will?'

I often get asked if I played against superstar x or superstar y in their formative years and whether I could tell if they were destined for greatness. And people are always interested in discovering whether I thought team-mates and opponents who should have gone on to greater things didn't. That isn't always because of their ability. A lot of other factors are at work. Sometimes it is down to the one thing no one can control: luck.

Was I ever good enough?

When team-mates came back from playing for England and I heard their stories of course I was jealous. Who wouldn't be? Every professional cricketer's ambition is to play for their country. Some realise fairly early that it's not going to happen, and they must scramble all their efforts into having a decent county career. Others will know quite quickly that they have a freakishly good talent that can get them all the way to the top if they stay fit.

Then there's the rest of us, the vast majority of county pros who have that fleeting moment in the sun and end up thinking what might have been.

Initially, I was in the first category. The coach and captain at my first county weren't 100% sure I'd be good enough, but they took a punt on me, and it paid off. So, for the first three or four years of my career all I wanted to do was play for as long as possible and get paid nicely and win trophies. My focus for probably the first few years was solely on getting into the team and keeping my spot.

My outlook changed when I got capped. As well as a pay rise, it meant a bit more job security. I was no longer worrying whether my contract will be renewed. I started looking forward. I could start to widen my horizons. I began to play with more freedom, and for three or four years I was ultra-consistent in all formats. That is when I thought I might be good enough to make the step up to international cricket. One or two nice things were written about me and a few TV commentators began to blow smoke up my arse, especially when I played one-day cricket.

But playing for England did not occupy my thoughts for long, a season or two at most. I looked around the circuit and could name 50 players similarly talented to me who had not had a sniff. Then I got a phone call from James Whitaker, who was one of the England selectors at the time.

Life with the Lions

There were no tears, no wild celebrations when I got chosen for the Lions. Just a sense of pride and a feeling that, you know what, I fucking deserve this. I had been churning out performances for three or four years. This wasn't some selectorial hunch.

When I met up with the other players in the squad there were two groups. Those of us who, like me, hoped it was the next stage towards being an England player, and the rest of the squad for whom this was merely the next part of that process, a stepping stone. My county coach would have been tearing his hair out trying to get a team spirit going amongst us. There was none. Even for the two weeks I was there, I never experienced such a weird dynamic. It was pretty ruthless, nearly everyone was there for themselves. They couldn't give a fuck whether you got runs or took wickets or, I imagine, if England won or not.

In the games I played I did OK, nothing outstanding but I certainly didn't look out of place. The opposition, the second-tier players from a mid-ranking Test nation, were not strong opponents. I have played harder games of county cricket many times.

I took it all in, tried to learn from the coaches and even other players, especially those I thought had that mental toughness the top players all possess. A few of my team-mates in that squad did make it. One or two

I knew straight away would. Others, with comparable records to mine, or in a couple of cases worse, got their chance with me too.

Regrets? Not really. In fact, I am quite proud of my reaction when I knew at the end of those two weeks that this was as good as it was going to get for me. Maybe I should have pushed harder and there might have been a happy ending, but the more I thought about it the more I realised I was happier not spending the rest of my career chasing that dream.

The Next Big Thing

In nearly 20 years I have seen far more players with good reputations at the age of 19 crash and burn than go on to have brilliant careers. In fact, if you really pushed me I can probably only think of two players who I knew instinctively could go all the way when I played against them for the first time.

One was Joe Root, who I encountered in a game at Headingley and spent the next few days raving about, until one of my team-mates told me to 'stop going on about that fucking Joe Root'. He just looked the real deal, technically good and resilient, which all prodigies need to be because there is nothing an experienced county fast bowler loves more than putting the Next Big Thing in his place. You're up against 30- to 35-year-olds who know what they are doing. Their skills are honed, they can spot a weakness in a 20-year-old straight away and they will ruthlessly exploit it. We had a few playing for us against Yorkshire that week, but by the end of the game even they admitted 'fucking Joe Root' was something special.

The other was Chris Woakes. A different type of player, of course, and not perhaps as naturally gifted. What impressed me was that he ran in as hard in his third and fourth spells as he did with the new ball. And he played with a smile on his face, he looked as if he was enjoying it. He still does, which is some achievement when you think of the sacrifices he's made to have the career he has, and the knockbacks he's had along the way.

I really feel for young players who come into county cricket already having a reputation. They had good raps in the press, enjoyed a prolific schools career and played for England Under-19s. One to Watch. The Next Big Thing. But if you look over the years at the England Under-19 teams, it's amazing how few of them go all the way to the top and play Test cricket. A lot of them fall by the wayside after a couple of years in county cricket.

If I read about the Next Big Thing I'm always quite excited to play against them but, often, the reality is somewhat different. They walk out with the demeanour of a dormouse. I remember a tubby left-hander at Derbyshire who was supposed to be the Next Big Thing. Well, we could have had eight slips and a gully for him, and he wouldn't have scored a run.

But then there are guys like Daryl Mitchell, who had no build-up whatsoever. We played against Worcestershire and this tubby little kid came out to open the batting and straight away I thought 'this guy's going to make millions of runs'. And he has, he ought to have played for England in my opinion, but he plays for an unfashionable county so that counts against him, or maybe he hasn't been on Sky enough.

I have a lot of sympathy for players who get thrust into the England limelight when they are still in their teens or early 20s. No player is fully developed at that age. There are freaks like Zak Crawley, who already looks the real deal, but what about someone like Haseeb Hameed? He can always say he played Test cricket, but I bet if he'd been allowed to find his feet and know more about his game he would be opening for England regularly by now, instead of trying to find a way back with his second county.

Big or small, does it matter?

At my first county, we didn't have a lot of international players. When we enjoyed a bit of success a couple got picked for England but quite often I would look around our dressing-room and could name half a dozen who were far better players than those from other clubs who did get the chance to play for their country.

I am not so sure these days if playing for a bigger county like Surrey, Lancashire or Yorkshire does make a difference at all, although it might accelerate the process because the bigger clubs tend to play in the first division of the Championship, against a better standard of opposition. Mind you, having experienced both in recent years, the gap between the two divisions has narrowed. Or standards in Division One have fallen. Anyway, you don't tend to see many selectors at second-division games.

There are a few examples of where playing for a big county can make the difference. I would say the majority of county pros regard Glamorgan's Chris Cooke as a better one-daykeeper-batsman than Ben Foakes. But one isn't quite as fashionable and plays for Glamorgan, while the other is at arguably the biggest county in the country with someone like Alec Stewart, who has a massive profile in the game, taking every opportunity to talk him up in his role as their director of cricket. Stats-wise they are similar, so there must be something that gets one selected above the other? Foakes has shown how good he is in his limited international career, but Brown may never get the chance. It shows how careers can have many 'sliding doors' moments which define us.

Would you call Somerset a smaller county? Even though they have been in Division One for years and are often challenging for honours. Yet how many of their players have broken through for England in that time? After Tom Banton, I'm struggling to name anyone.

Look at James Hildreth, who averages 42 and has been one of the most consistent batsmen of the past 15 years, but who has never been picked by England. If you polled the 400 county cricketers in England today and asked who the best player was in their generation not to be selected, he would be top of 99% of players' lists. When you think of the players who have played for England during his time – Adam Lyth, Nick Compton, Sam Robson, Joe Denly for example – when he hasn't, it's staggering. And I don't mean that disrespectfully to those four, but they are not quite in Hildreth's class stats wise.

Should a player's age be a factor? A few weeks after I played for England Lions I asked a selector what my chances of going on that winter's Lions tour were and he told me that they didn't want to take anyone over 30. Fair enough, so I did find it amusing when Joe Denly got his Test call-up at the age of 32 in 2019.

Joe is an excellent player who has had a few years in the England set-up and made some good contributions. I think plenty of players would look back at their careers and wonder 'what if' a selector had favoured them above others who did get the chance to play when the differences between us were minimal.

Back to Hildreth. You might argue he should have moved to a 'bigger' county. But why should he? I would love to know the reasons why a succession of selectors ignored a batsman who consistently performed at such a high level. One argument might be that he's played half of his games at Taunton, which for years was a better batting wicket than, say, Durham, until Dom Bess and Jack Leach came along and they started to prepare spin-friendly pitches.

Years ago, England coach Duncan Fletcher backed a hunch on Marcus Trescothick when he was averaging in the low-20s and it paid off spectacularly. These days the approach to selection and recruitment, as I will come on to later, is more statistics-based and analytical. Does, say, Hildreth have that much better a record on flat pitches at Taunton and the Oval than he does at the Riverside or Derby? A couple of clicks of the analyst's mouse and you can find out. It shouldn't matter if you play for The Moon CC. The figures don't lie.

It's easier to get picked for England's white-ball teams simply because there are more T20 and one-day internationals than Test matches, and these days only a handful of players will play in all three formats to protect them from burnout.

If you're regularly getting to the knockout stages of one-day competitions or T20 Finals Day selectors and the media will look more closely at that county's players, even if they are not playing for the big clubs. Pat Brown is a classic recent example of that. A relative unknown whose county started to do well in white-ball cricket on the back of his performances and he got picked by England. If your team is successful, its size shouldn't matter. But if your club is small and is not successful then it's going to be hard. When was the last time a Derbyshire player was selected for England?

The fallout

When a player comes back to his county from England duty it's his team-mates and coaches who have to deal with the fallout, whether said player is now a bona fide superstar or has returned with his tail between his legs and the knowledge that his shot at the big time has come and gone.

I have seen both sides; players who have really thrived playing for England and others for whom the experience probably cost them two years of their careers while they recovered mentally from not being considered good enough and rediscovered the form that earned them the opportunity.

The one thing they all have in common, something that they all have strong views on, is the level of scrutiny they are under. There aren't too many players like Kevin Pietersen who seem to thrive on the attention. There can't be too many downsides to playing international cricket, but I imagine knowing that the replay of your dismissal has been shown five times before you've even made it back to the dressing-room must be one.

Every pundit and even a few members of the coaching staff will have an opinion on your technique if you don't perform. That comes with the territory. It becomes an issue when the player goes back to his county and is convinced that the technique which got him to that level in the first place needs changing because it may have been exposed, without sometimes realising that there was always a chance of that happening because the standard is so much better than they are used to. They will change things and are shocked that it doesn't improve their performances in county cricket, not least because now they are an England player they are a marked man and the opposition are going to raise their game against them.

Others come back from international cricket and their views of county cricket change, whether they have been successful or not for their country. The pitches are suddenly crap and the practice facilities are shit. And, compared to international cricket, they are. This constant whingeing can have a detrimental effect on the team. You welcome back your superstar player expecting him to win even more games for you and find that his motivation, now he has reached the promised land, has disappeared.

It's incredibly frustrating, but I can understand why it happens. They now regard themselves as international players, so why put yourself out? Not many bowlers in that situation are going to perform at full tilt for their county and risk injury if there's an England game coming up. They might bowl three or four overs at top speed, but then they drop down the gears or get you a nice 40 and get out. I remember hearing on the circuit from several players of a star batsman going back to his county and flattering to deceive on many occasions. 'Sorry lads,' he'd say as he undid his pads. 'It wasn't testing me. I was fucking bored.'

To be honest, players in that situation might as well just rest or do a bit of work in the nets. It doesn't motivate them, whereas the opportunity to play would motivate a young player or someone who feels they deserve a chance in the first team.

Even in second-team cricket more damage will be done playing someone who just isn't interested. It's another instance when clear communication lines with a coach can be very important.

Others will come back and realise that they aren't quite good enough for that level and just get on with it. This is where I think cricket is so good. When you live in each other's pockets for half a year you do develop relationships. You won't like everyone in your team but if a mate gets the chance to play for England you feel almost as proud of them as they are, and you will help cushion the blow if it doesn't work out.

6

Pressure

MENTAL HEALTH has been a major issue in county cricket for a while now, and while the ECB are much more aware of it than they were when I started playing, I believe there is still a long way to go.

The books written by Marcus Trescothick, Luke Sutton and Mike Yardy were avidly consumed in the dressing-room when they came out. Both were painfully honest, and I think any county pro who read either of them would recognise the issues they faced and sympathise wholly with both players. A lot would have thought 'something like that happened to me'.

During my career, I reckon around 10–20 of my team-mates at one time or another were suffering from some form of depression. Now, there is obviously a big difference between being pissed off because you're not playing well, or you've been dropped, and feeling that the world is caving in on you. It can be very hard for players to differentiate between the two, especially during the season when it's pretty relentless and there is so little opportunity to sit and reflect.

I would say on average two or three times a year a team-mate has confided in me that he was struggling and needed a break from the game. You might be playing in a team which is winning trophies, but if you can't buy a run or your best balls are getting hit for four then being in a successful environment will not help your state of mind.

You would sometimes see players doing well who were struggling; it could be the added pressure of England selection, contract negotiations or family issues which would take away the personal satisfaction from what should have been an enjoyable run of form.

I have always tried to be a positive presence in the squads I have been in. I have a decent level of perspective and can empathise with other people and what they are facing on a day-to-day basis through my own experiences.

Some would argue that someone as positive and level-headed as me wouldn't and didn't suffer from any issues. The fact is I haven't struggled with full blown depression, and I am extremely fortunate to have played for a long time without experiencing too many tough times. But on one occasion I was treated so badly by my club it really affected me and I had a panic attack while out shopping two days later. At the time I brushed it off, but eventually I realised that the way I had been treated and the lack of empathy afterwards had a detrimental effect on me.

Thankfully, I was proactive in speaking to the right people through the Professional Cricketers' Association, we managed to get control of it quickly, and it hasn't been a long-term issue for me. But when the stakes are so high and our careers and reputations are on the line, we can very quickly be affected by those around us. This probably relates to my attitudes towards player care and the quality of management within professional sport.

I have really strong views about the after-care of cricketers and sportsmen and women once their careers are over and how they should be better managed.

Cricketers have to accept early in their career that the outside world will judge them on the number of runs scored, wickets taken and averages. For bowlers, the currency is wickets, five-fors and ten-fors. And there have been some highs. I have scored lots of runs and taken plenty of wickets, some of them match-winning efforts, but the innings I tend to remember most are the ones when I battled away to get a score when I didn't know where my next run was coming from, or found a way to do a job with the ball when I felt crap.

To the outside world, it's irrelevant if you got a shit decision from an umpire, the ball rolled along the ground because the pitch was crap, or you beat the outside edge 15 times, but couldn't get the batsman to nick off. It still says you got nought or had figures of 18-1-84-0 in the paper or on Cricinfo. You get used to comments, even from friends, like, 'Any danger of you scoring a run?' 'You're going to get dropped soon' or 'I thought you could play.' You even get used to walking down the road imagining that people just going about their normal lives are staring and pointing, saying, 'There's TSC, I see he got another nought yesterday.'

Every professional will experience this at some stage in their career, most of us quite regularly.

I'm talking about the days when you pull back the curtains in the morning and say a silent prayer that the forecasters have got it right and it's going to be raining for 12 hours solid. No chance of playing, no chance of getting another duck or bowling like a muppet and confirmation that you've had another bad day. Thank God for that.

The problems start when, as well as judging yourself harshly as a cricketer, you begin to think you're a shit person as well. I have experienced this and it affected my relationships with my parents, wife and family. I would withdraw from people and nobody would know how to talk to me. It's like a bereavement when everyone avoids the subject. Then you'd compound your problems by looking at your Twitter or Instagram feed and reading comments about how crap you are. And you'd be tempted to reply, 'You went to work in an office today, you got paid so who is really judging you when you walk down the street or go to your local club for a quiet pint?' A positive outlook on life isn't much good in those situations, but we're all different.

Professional athletes are funny creatures; we find ways to cope with situations that amateurs may or may not be able to comprehend. Every day you walk out on to the field to be judged, as a batter you have the chance to score a hundred, a bowler has the chance to take five wickets and walk off the field to a standing ovation.

As a fielder you can take the match-winning catch or stop the boundary that enables your team to win the game. You could do any of those things … or you could miss the first ball and watch your mates smash it everywhere on a flat pitch, bowl a shower of shit with the new ball and let the opposition score 150 too many or – and this is one of the worst feelings – you could drop their best player who goes on to make a hundred and every run feels like a pin prick to your eyes!

There are plenty of occasions when you sit in the changing-room after a day's play and want the ground to swallow you up. You just want to get to the safety of home where you can hide away, at least until it all starts again tomorrow.

If that all sounds a bit morbid, let's flip it round and talk about those times when you are invincible and you walk down the road feeling 8ft tall and in your head you think that everyone is talking about how bloody good you are and all the coffee shops you haunt want to give you a free latte.

I remember once finishing 110 not out in a Championship game. I raised my bat when I got to 100, I raised it again when I walked off and I knew that I'd be getting the same adulation again the next day, regardless of whether I made 110 or 510. My wife and I went out for a three-course meal, drank loads of expensive wine and I slept the best I'd slept in ages. I knew the next day would be a success. It is one of the few days – they probably number in single figures – in a career spanning nearly 20 years that I still remember now and will probably never forget. Incidentally, I got out for 115 in the second over of the day, but the crowd gave me another standing ovation.

But when you're out of nick and can't buy a run then being dropped is a relief, and don't let any player tell you otherwise. Once you start having a bad trot your mindset changes very quickly. That's what differentiates great players from average ones. Great players get over it quicker, they have a level of trust in their own ability that us mere mortals, in other words 95% of county players, don't possess.

One thing I would say is, any player who has a long and successful career in county cricket is a tough cookie. The guys who play international cricket for many years are obviously a cut above skill and mentality wise, but the county players who never earn the big bucks but churn out performances day to day should not be discounted.

I remember a top Australian international telling me once that county cricket was tougher than international cricket on the pitch. Having to play day-in, day-out at empty grounds on tough pitches without any preparation time was something he couldn't grasp, especially with the added issue of media scrutiny on top.

Players with the mental strength to ride the rough periods are the ones that will succeed over a long period of time. Look at Paul Collingwood, Ian Bell and Matt Prior, who were dropped by England and shredded to pieces in the media but came back and never got dropped again. After that they became world class.

The ability to pull out a score when you need it probably determines if you have a brilliant or an average career.

I remember a team-mate getting a tap on the shoulder from the coach to say he'd been dropped before a game against Glamorgan. Honestly, it was the happiest he'd been for months. We went out to play football in the warm-up and he performed like a mixture of Lionel Messi and Usain Bolt, running around like a madman and producing all manner of skills.

Being dropped and accepting failure does get a bit easier the older you are, but when you're young knowing how to deal with it so you can come back a better player is tougher than improving the technical issues that might have cost you your spot in the first place.

Like I said, I've scored plenty of runs and taken lots of wickets in my career, but I remember more innings when I battled like fuck to get 40 or 50 when I was out of nick. I was under the cosh and I turned it around and found something. That's probably why I was pretty successful in my career, I dealt with those situations and got through them instead of getting to a point and falling off a cliff, which is what happens to a lot of players when form deserts them and they don't know how to grind it out.

Do I think clubs do enough to look after the mental health of players? It's better than it was, but there is still a long way to go. This is elite performance sport remember. We can call upon two or three physiotherapists, a couple of strength and conditioning coaches and sometimes three or four technical coaches, yet the sports psychologist is usually part-time. Counties look after the physical stuff because a six-pack is visible evidence of personal improvement. For example, in the winter, everyone is in the gym all the time but how much time is spent on wellbeing? Very little. It's assumed that because we're not playing we're not suffering, but those pressures are never too far away. Even one bad winter net session can leave you feeling shit for days.

I have spoken to a few players on the circuit who have suffered from mental illness and they said their counties were brilliant when they were diagnosed with depression. The PCA have an excellent helpline which can put you straight in touch with a specialist or sometimes, as has happened to me, you can have a quiet word with your coach when a team-mate confides in you that he is struggling.

Fortunately, most current county coaches played in an era when mental health started to become a serious issue. But if a coach is under pressure, his priority is not going to be your mental wellbeing; he will still be more concerned about how many runs you have made or wickets you have taken because that currency might decide whether he keeps his job or not. I would say significantly more players have failed in their careers because of their mental health rather than their physical or technical shortcomings. I don't think county clubs will be doing their best for their players until all 18 employ a full-time wellness coach.

I was so fortunate to forge such a strong relationship with the first sports psychologist I worked with in the early part of my career. We still talk now, and I think that being able to confide in someone without being judged is so important to staying healthy and happy.

A numbers game

The Holy Grail for batsmen: 100 runs. I often get asked if I walk out to bat on certain days convinced I'm going to get a big score. Honestly, you could count those occasions on one hand, and remember I've played for a decent length of time.

Going out thinking you're going to get nought? Now you're talking. It's much easier to get nought than a hundred. One mistake and you're gone. For top-order players it is always a bit harder as the bowlers are fresher and have a new ball. When I did bat up there it was horrible getting out and later realising how flat the pitch was and that I should have played differently. Batting lower down was more fun as you could set up your game based on what you had seen and the feedback from your top-order players. Invariably the bowlers were a bit more tired and the ball a bit softer, which I think we all enjoy. To score a hundred probably takes around four to five hours. That is a lot of time when you cannot afford to make a mistake, so the concentration required is intense.

I was listening to Dominic Sibley a while back saying he only felt settled after facing 30 balls. Which probably explains why he's now playing for England. I never felt truly settled until I'd got 70 runs, never mind faced 70 balls. That may seem quite a high number, but I reckon most county batsmen would say something similar.

Perversely, sometimes, the longer I batted, the worse I got. It might sound daft, but the first few balls I faced were always my best because my mind was usually clear. The danger with batting is that sometimes you get in and start thinking too far ahead. I would often face as few as four balls and think to myself 'I'm feeling good today' and then nick off to the fifth when I could have left it alone. Top players talk about being 'in the moment', but I would say that feeling when I knew that whatever I did I was going to succeed only happened to me a handful of times in my career, including when I got my highest score. But it was only when I'd got to 70-odd, or batted for, say, a session and a half, that I knew I would only have myself to blame if I got out.

Because we play each other so often in England, it's fairly easy to spot a player who is in good nick and likely to make you suffer if you don't get him out early. During my career the one player who stood out in that regard was Stuart Law, who played for Lancashire and Essex and who now coaches Middlesex. Bloody hell, once he got to 15 or had batted for 45 minutes you knew you were fucked. The same applied to Mark Ramprakash. We'd have a team meeting when we played Middlesex or Surrey and the discussion would be if we could keep him to 80 runs tops we'd be doing well. More recently, James Hildreth and Gary Ballance are two players who once in are very hard to shift.

Players who can play those long, grinding innings are fewer now. A lot more one-day shots are employed against the red ball and younger batsmen seem happy to get 60 off 40 balls and spend the time when they might have been pushing on towards a century in the nets, honing the one-day shots that might earn them a franchise gig in the winter.

In a roundabout way I was a bit like that. When I started every season my aim was to average 40 or more. So, if I got to 80 in the first innings I felt I'd hit my target and the runs I scored above that would be really helpful for the team. If I got to 120, that equated to not having to worry if my next innings ended on nought. I had those runs in the bank. Believe me, mine is not an unusual mindset for a county batsman. It's probably why I didn't have a career like Joe Root or Ian Bell, but it puts me in a good position to understand how mere mortals work which has definitely helped me when speaking to younger players and trying to understand how they are thinking.

I have my own flaws which is why I am who I am. I still worked my nuts off to be the best I could be and to do the best job I possibly could for the team; I just didn't have the ability to score bucket-loads of runs year-in, year-out like the top guys. Very few county cricketers do.

I never found enjoying a team-mate's success difficult. If there were beers in the changing-room afterwards I'd always stay for one, even if I'd got nothing that day. But it was hard not to be jealous, too, especially if they had enjoyed better conditions and faced tired bowlers. I always respected players who got the runs which won the game, the grafting 60 as an opener or someone who saw off their best bowler when he was at his most dangerous, not just the batter who scores his runs on a flat one when the bowlers are knackered or can't take wickets with the old ball.

Good coaches began to identify more clearly players who were doing a good job for the team and would often highlight them in team talks: the bloke bowling into the wind, up the hill taking 1-30 off 20 overs, or the batsman who faced 80 balls for his 20 runs but who enabled the No.6 to come in and smash a hundred against a worn-out attack. The players who get to a hundred always get the headlines, but the best teams I've played for appreciated those who did the shitty jobs, without getting external recognition.

For the first half of my career when it came to the end-of-the-season contract talks most coaches and CEOs, faced with two days of non-stop negotiations with expectant players and their agents, tended to concentrate on your number of runs and wickets rather than how you got them. Early-season matches in the Parks or Fenner's, when you cashed in against student bowling, were a great way of fattening your average before the season proper even started.

But then analysts became more prevalent and were able to present coaches with in-depth statistical work. They knew if you scored runs at a ground which had poor pitches and a lot of low-scoring games, or if you got a hundred when the game was consigned to a draw and the opposition opening batsman was turning his arm over. In short, they knew when you performed under more pressure.

Team-mates

When you spend so much time with the same group of people you have to make the effort to get on, even if it's a pretence sometimes. My phone book is full of names of blokes I have played with or against, literally hundreds of them. Some I may have only met or played against a couple of times, but who I bonded with, even if it was only for the duration of a match. 'Give us your number and let's keep in touch,' you say at the end of the game. But 95 times out of 100 you never do.

But you know what? I can scroll through my phone, look at a name and invariably each one will evoke a happy memory. That bowler who got me out a couple of times in the same game, but who I discovered shared the same somewhat world-weary view of our game as me when he came over with us to the sponsors' box for a drink after play one night.

It's no different to any workplace I suppose, except that for more than half the year you spend more time with the same group of 20 blokes than you do with your wife or any family member. You can form a very intense bond with someone very quickly. The new signing from another county, the gun overseas player who you've always admired and thought, 'I bet he's a nice bloke, I wouldn't mind being friends with him.' When he turns up, you make that bit of an extra effort. A night out, a few beers, an invitation to a barbecue at your place and suddenly you're mates.

I've been with players when they get picked for England and others when they lose their contracts, you see all the highs and lows, and the older and more experienced I got the more I was approached by younger lads looking for advice. They might ask me which agent to sign with, or where to go in the winter. That role I always enjoyed because it is great to pass on what you have learnt to help a mate. Generally, cricketers are a good bunch who look after one another, it's a close community and 99.9% of us recognise how lucky we are to be involved in this brilliant game.

It's not as dog-eat-dog as football has become, I guess because there's less money involved but also because a lot of us grew up together and have known each other a long time. There aren't many sports where you can play against someone for your county as a ten-year-old and still be on opposite sides 25 years later in the Championship.

But sometimes you can try too hard. There have been plenty of overseas players I felt I should get to know better. I've admired the way they played, liked the way they looked. Your expectations of them are unrealistic and when they turn out to be a bit of a twat you start wondering if you are the solid judge of character you thought you were.

It can work both ways. Sometimes you would see a player on TV and make a judgement. He might look like a keen bean on the pitch and you think he's going to be a badger who goes to bed at 8pm and hates fun. But then you play a season with them and they happen to be the most sociable bloke in the world. That is what makes it so much fun playing with different teams and meeting new people.

Some of these relationships can be quite intense; it's a bit like falling in love for the first time. You go on a Lions tour or play in a franchise tournament and bond with someone you haven't even played against in an instant. But it is a little illusory if I'm honest. The thing I have learnt during my career is that you can make a lot of friends, but only a handful are friends for life, and sometimes that happens when you hardly play with them at all.

Of my five best friends in cricket is someone I only played with once and that was for my club when he was the overseas pro. That was 20-odd years ago, but we're in touch all the time; I spoke to him this morning funnily enough. I played twice with the chairman of my old club and we've been mates now for 15 years. When I played club cricket in the southern hemisphere at the start of my career I struck up a couple of friendships which have endured over the years. You might think there's a pattern forming here. What about the guys he played with all that time? Well, the truth is there are probably only seven or eight who I would describe as really close friends and who I will invite to my 60th birthday party.

If you put 20 adults in the same room and tell them they are effectively going to be living together for six months there is no way they are all going to get on. As I've said, cricketers generally are an amenable, sociable bunch. We learn that because we spend so much time together we need to at least try and tolerate each other. But even if everyone does – and in my experience there are always a couple of odd characters – it makes no difference to whether you are successful or not.

Every miserable git in the team will be cut some slack if they can bang out 1,200 runs or take 80 wickets season after season. For all the mumbo jumbo that's spoken about 'creating a cohesive environment' (incidentally, this is a phrase trotted out by every coach there ever was) it's about having good players. You can't turn a bunch of average players into a winning machine, simply because cricket is an individual sport in a team environment.

Let's look at Derbyshire over the past 20 years as an example. I've heard lots of good things about the dressing-room environment there. They might have had the best, most hard-working bunch of lads around but they haven't won anything because they haven't got enough match-winners in their squad. That's how clubs create successful eras, they build the foundations through hard work and graft, but ensure the right players are brought in to give them the X factor that wins trophies.

In the same way that you might only form a handful of really close friendships, I can honestly say that in nearly 20 years I have only ever come across two or three real dickheads in county cricket. One of them genuinely did not want his team-mates to do well, as I discovered when I got my first hundred for my new county. It was an emotional moment for me, and a lot of the guys knew how much it meant.

All except one, who didn't even begrudgingly offer his congratulations or stay for a beer to celebrate. We hardly spoke for the next four or five years. I don't rate him as a human being.

But that is rare. When you think about the many different backgrounds and routes into the game that a squad of 20 cricketers take to get to the dressing-room you are now sharing, it does sometimes make me wonder how there tends to be peace and harmony. In one team you might have seven different nationalities and 15 different upbringings. One year I played in a team with a West Indian, a South African, two Pakistanis and a farmer – a real melting pot. Most teams are not made up of ten middle-class, white, public-school-educated males anymore and that is what makes it such a great environment to spend your time in.

It is fascinating how you do end up getting along. What makes Dan Lawrence, who's a bit rogue and likes a cigarette after play, get on with the gentleman farmer and run machine Alastair Cook? Every dressing-room needs a couple of oddballs. Guys like Northamptonshire spinner Graeme White, who took himself off to India for five months to explore the country on his own and play a very basic level of club cricket.

It's such good preparation for life after cricket. If you can get on with the meditating, vegan, spiritualist as well as the near-alcoholic, chain-smoking cockney git then you can prosper in any environment.

7

Coaching and Coaches

LIKE PLAYERS, there are good coaches and there are bad coaches. Most English pros will work with quite a few from the moment they join their county's junior pathway until they retire. And in my experience, if you can form a trusting relationship with even one or two during your career you will have done well.

In my time, a couple stand out. One I first worked with when I was in the junior set-up at one of the counties I played for and another who, after a fine career at the highest level as a player, made the successful transition into coaching.

The guy I have known for the best part of 30 years – let's call him Coach 1 – was still offering me little bits of advice when he was long past his retirement age. We hadn't worked one-on-one for a few years, but he was watching me play during a game which was on Sky and spotted that my stance wasn't right. He called me the next day, the conversation lasted about 30 seconds. 'Hi TSC, you OK? Anyway, you need to sort your set-up out, it's not balanced.' That was all he had to say. No need for any more. And because I had worked with him for so long I trusted him implicitly. Next day, I went into the nets with the coach at my county, adopted a more upright stance and the runs began to flow again.

Coach 2 was much younger and went into it after a stellar playing career. I respected him for what he'd achieved as a player, but initially I was sceptical about whether he could help me. But he had absolutely no ego – which, as I'll explain, is a trait in the best coaches – and all he was interested in was helping me improve. He came into my life when I felt I was probably at my peak and the things we worked on helped push my game to new levels. I consider it one of the best things about my career that I had access to those two great coaches among others. They may have come from different generations, but the beauty was that they actually coached in exactly the same way.

Look, the basics of cricket have never changed, it's just how they are interpreted. The problems start when coaches think they have to reinvent the wheel, or they let their ego take over. For example, when I went into the nets after that tip from Coach 1 about my stance my county coach could have pushed back, but he was happy that I had helped solve my own problem. I've come across a few coaches who have felt marginalised when their own methods have been challenged, or they thought their views were being ignored. Nearly all of them are generally ineffective and could not build strong relationships with players over a long period. If there is one thing worse than a player with a bruised ego, it's a coach with one.

Good reputations don't make good coaches. Fact

One of the top coaches in the world once implied that a coach can do more damage by saying something than by keeping quiet and observing. I have seen coaches rush towards me after I'd faced two balls in the nets. How can they create a balanced judgement on my game and offer helpful advice at that moment in my career on the basis of such flimsy evidence?

So many coaches hate the sound of silence, especially if they have played at the top level and have been around the block a bit. The biggest barrier is trust. I don't want to name names in this case, but during my formative years there was a coach who worked with many young cricketers as a consultant, employed by the ECB. Consultant coaches can have a great impact because sometimes hearing a different perspective is refreshing, but a coach needs to build a relationship with the player before diving in with his or her often one-size-fits-all method on cricket.

In one week this 'consultant' managed to ruin about five players' careers for the next five years. I was lucky enough to be invited to a training camp with this coach, and before we had even started in the nets he sat us down and told us how we had to bowl, with what action and how long it would take. 'Brilliant' everyone thought. We are going to be living our dreams on the world stage and this is the first step. The truth is that I don't think any of that group made it to international cricket and very few got as far as the professional game. I was one of the lucky ones, but it took me months to recover and I vowed never to let a coach ruin me again.

Within a couple of weeks of working with this coach my confidence was shot to pieces and I was swiftly demoted to my club's second team. I couldn't even do a long barrier on the third-man boundary without it going through my legs for four as the opposition (and probably a few team-mates) pissed themselves laughing.

It can be so tough when a big name comes in to work with you as a young player. You might not agree with them but what are you supposed to say when they tell you to change your whole game five minutes after meeting you? 'Fuck off mate, what do you know?' You are an impressionable young player and trying to impress. I think the first responsibility of players who might have had a decent career and are now masquerading as coaches is to take as long as it takes to really get to know the players. A coach who is willing to spend time working out what the player needs in order to improve has to be confident and believe in their ability to help. My bullshit detector goes off the scale when I meet a coach, who is usually an ex-pro, trying to make a career out of some crackpot coaching theory they believe in. The older you get, the longer it takes to build trust in a coach.

The best have spent time learning their craft alongside more experienced coaches, they take the opportunity to get to know you and don't jump in at the first shit shot or loose delivery. Every time I experienced this I immediately put a block up. Don't treat all players the same, that way you can build an effective relationship. I always thought if a new coach came in and gave me space and time I would end up going to him, then the door opens for them to help you. Doing it the other way round can cause more harm than good in my experience.

I can proudly say that since my younger years I have never blamed a coach for my failings. I will speak to them about my game, but when it comes down to your success or otherwise, it is on you. If I see a player go straight to the laptop after getting out it raises the question 'do you need to get out, watch it and ask a coach for a solution?' This relates back to good coaches. Can they allow the player to make the decisions in the middle, coach themselves during the event rather than fucking it up and then trying to find a solution? Great players like Stuart Broad or Jimmy Anderson for instance may not get it right all the time, but they will identify and correct any problems pretty quickly, which can usually be the difference between winning or losing.

Good coaches become friends for life and the trust you build lasts forever. I count myself fortunate to have worked with some great ones, and maybe a bit unfortunate that I wasted time with some of the rubbish ones as well. The good ones care about you as a person. I've seen coaches cry when telling a player he is dropped, they cared more about the player's feelings than the fact they hadn't been performing well. That is why when a coach is under pressure their worst traits show. If you are losing and still treat your players with respect and care you will do for the vast majority of county players. To see a coach pass his stress on to players and forget they are humans is always a red flag.

Catching them young

Most county coaches don't do a lot of pure coaching with their players for the simple reason that the majority of senior professionals don't need it. Their games will need some fine-tuning now and again, but the key is to make them feel sufficiently challenged and supported.

Sure, they might spot a technical flaw occasionally which a player works on, but a lot of the time that is first picked up by analysts, who play an increasingly important role in the county game. And once that flaw is spotted, it doesn't take a player long to rectify it, usually a net session or two.

For most modern coaches in England, their role is more about player management, facilitating and often counselling, areas where former international players tend to be strong because of the top-level experiences they have had. Some of them are very good simply because they can create the right environment for their players to flourish.

How we structure our coaching in England is an interesting point. The best-paid and highest-level coaches will be with the county's first-team squad, leading a team of five or six working with the players on training and match days. You turn up at an under-14 game and there are two lower level coaches trying to organise everything and make the tea as well. These people are brilliant, they do a huge amount of work and don't get paid very much for the pleasure. But this is the most important time for a player's development. The parent or volunteer who scraped through his level 2 and gets a county tracksuit is invaluable in their own way, but he or she isn't going to help develop the steady production line that most counties need to sustain themselves, especially in the wake of Covid-19 when playing budgets will be squeezed. These people have a role to play but it is about putting the right people in the right places.

Look at what brilliant county academies such as Surrey, Somerset and Worcestershire have produced consistently over the years for their first team. Imagine if you put a Peter Moores or Paul Farbrace with the 13 to 17-year-olds lower down the food chain and paid them properly. I would be amazed if you didn't have seven or eight homegrown players in the team within five years. The counties that have been doing this for a few years are seeing the results, and it won't be long before it becomes the norm. Look at some of the coaches working in Premier League football academies. Stick someone like Nicky Butt alongside some experienced coaches and the rewards will come.

We see players come on to county staff at 17 or 18 and they are so far off the pace it is not surprising that within two years most of them are scrapping for their careers and looking at other options. The importance of those vital formative years before they join the professional staff makes a mockery of the investment that goes into the coaching at the younger age groups.

The encouraging news is that I think this attitude is starting to slowly change, and we are seeing higher-profile coaches starting to work more within the junior systems.

The first counties to really invest in this will reap the rewards, especially smaller clubs who have to build their strategies around this just to compete with the counties playing at international grounds who have the financial resources to recruit the best players.

Going private

Not all aspiring young cricketers can afford to go to independent schools, and if counties acted a bit smarter they could make more use of the private system to nurture and improve young players.

I was looking through one of the cricket magazines at the end of 2020 and they had a glossy supplement about schools cricket with as many pages as the magazine itself. They detailed the very impressive cricket facilities at a hundred fee-paying and junior prep schools for boys and girls and reading the names of the coaching staff at these places was like going back in time to my own career. 'Christ, I got out to him once' and 'I remember bowling him for a duck.' So many of these masters of cricket or coaches at the best schools are former county pros who have become coaches in their own right because nearly all their experience is working with youngsters at an impressionable age. And in a lot of cases their schools offer facilities as good and in some cases better than their local county club.

So why don't counties set up formal links with some of them and establish mini-hubs if you like? In geographically large counties it makes a lot more sense for young players to go somewhere ten miles away two or three times a week rather than making the 50-mile round trip by taxi (paid for by the county) which one young pro I know did every week from his private school to his county's indoor nets during the winter, when his own school had perfectly good facilities at his disposal next door.

It might also encourage more youngsters from state schools, where cricket provision is virtually non-existent now, and those whose only have access to cricket through their local club, with limited practice facilities, or whose parents have neither the time nor the money to drive long distances so their offspring can practise. It would also be a great selling point for private schools, in a very competitive market, to be aligned, even loosely, with a county's established junior coaching pathway.

I can only guess the thing which is holding counties back would be the negative reaction of their own coaches, who might not want to cede control, or even trust those working at private schools, even if the vast majority will have just as much experience in coaching and playing professionally.

Let's talk about PowerPoint

Picture the scene. A coach walks into a room full of highly motivated individuals from all over the world who have all had different experiences and journeys to this point. They all want to win (the bonuses are far better) and they all want to take wickets, or score runs to play for their country (again, because the money is better). I have been in this situation many times. The coach will talk to them with a 40-slide PowerPoint presentation about how he wants the team to play. This may work for a short period of time, but in county cricket we eat, sleep and live together for seven months of the year and the environment created will make this time either heaven or hell.

If a coach can create an environment to suit that set of individuals they have a great chance, but it shouldn't be purely down to what the coach wants. The best coaches empower players and allow the squad to create the environment which will enable them to have ownership of the team culture they are living in.

It may be what the coach wants, but the skill of getting the players to own that is something I have seen on only a few occasions. Across all sports, I don't think we have seen many dictatorships work in recent times. Players can think for themselves, and when they are on the pitch this is what wins games and tournaments, not overcontrolling coaches who do not want to pass over responsibility to their players at the right time.

Save me from FADS

I am all for developing myself and learning new things to improve as a person and as a sportsperson. If I can see a relevance, but most importantly a consistency, in an activity I will commit to it fully to improve on a personal level and help the team.

But Mr Chief Executive, do not spend your club's hard-earned money on some fad to which we all commit our time and then never speak about again until the end-of-season piss-up when we all laugh about the 'expert' who had us falling backwards into each other's arms with a blindfold on, or breathing into a bag and checking our heart rates that March afternoon in the committee-room.

Committee-rooms in pavilions are useful to players in certain ways:

Eating

Drinking

Drugs tests (probably not useful, but at least it serves a purpose)

So why have I spent so many hours sitting in these rooms between October and March doing the most ridiculous things known to man? The worst thing is these 'experts' are charging an extortionate rate to make a bunch of 20 pro cricketers look like idiots as they move around the room standing in different coloured squares or being told they are a different coloured animal. It's a cottage industry all of its own. Another favourite is the fabled personality test.

I would estimate 90% of these 'seminars' are a waste of money because once you leave the room everyone moves on and completely forgets about what they just did. The key thing in these situations is consistency. So many people come and go that it is the ones who the coach commits to that have the biggest impact. Fads are so common in sport as everyone searches for the golden nugget that takes the team to the top. My own observations, based on the top teams I have seen and played in, are:

Good players

Well-run club

Coaches who the players like and trust

A shared love (fitness/drinking/money) are all examples that can work

For me not enough coaches give the players time to have fun together. Don't spend £1,000 on someone waffling on about the benefits of floatation relaxation, instead go and buy a load of beers, some food and let the players unwind together, share some stories and create memories that will raise a smile and sustain team morale when times are tough.

I remember one psychologist made us balance on a piece of tape stretching from one end of the room to the other. Extrovert to introvert, you stood on the tape depending what you saw yourself as. Watching 30 players and coaches walking on this line, all looking at the bloke next to them and asking if they liked people more than them, left me scratching my head. It certainly didn't achieve as much as spending his fee on a few bottles of wine and a nice lunch in town.

I am still waiting for the day when a player says that the hour spent breathing into a paper bag in February contributed to his success in July. The more time I spent in overheated meeting rooms drinking tepid filter coffee the more I felt the time could be spent better elsewhere.

Sports psychologists are a vital part of a professional sports team for many reasons. They can offer great counsel to the coaching staff and players. A good sports psychologist is worth their weight in gold, but I believe coaches must commit to them and do their research before introducing them to the squad. Bring in someone who is too theory-driven and they can quite quickly lose the players they are trying to help. I've seen one psychologist last two sessions before being sent back to his university classroom. The best ones are there just when you need them, not when you are suddenly having a bad time. They appear and you go and have a chat about life, money, the weather, anything you want and you start to enjoy talking to them. Over time you reveal yourself to them so they can find out about you and help you overcome your problems.

Greater self-awareness is vital and the stuff I did throughout my career was helpful, the key word being 'throughout'. It was never a one-off or something I read on Facebook and thought 'I'll try that.' Believe me, there are many players who have.

The cricketing non-cricketer

Not all of us has a deep distrust of these cod psychologists. I call them 'non-cricketing cricketers'; guys who lap up all the peripheral stuff, who can tell an introvert from an extrovert and sail through personality tests. The trouble is, when it's time to play cricket on a cold April day and the ball is nipping around, no amount of mindfulness or Yo-Yo tests are going to stop a nip-backer thumping into your pads first ball. You depart to stony silence from the members with the first duck of the season in the ledger. Mentally, you might have gone out to bat feeling that you are in a 'good head space', but I would strongly argue that the hour spent on some fad might have been better spent in the nets or with the regular sports psychologist who, as I will mention, should be more full-time than part-time.

I don't think there is a sport like cricket for indulging people looking for the theory which is going to revolutionise the game but has never been explored before. The trouble is that a lot of players listen to all these crack theorists and lap it up, believing it can turn them into something they are not. In one dressing-room I was part of, the lads would have a bet on how many times a week, never mind during a season, one of our team-mates would start espousing some idea he'd read on the web or heard on a podcast. One year, I think we nearly made enough to cover something much more beneficial to him and us – a night out in the pub together.

The best coaches coach, nothing else

The minute a coach wants something from you as a player they are fucked. There is nothing wrong with a player who scores a hundred or takes five wickets and says it was because of the work he has done with his coach. That is an organic reaction, it's authentic.

Good coaches will be referenced by players in the media or recommended to team-mates, and even opponents, because of the work they have done to improve them. The rewards for the coach will follow, whether it's a better job at a bigger club or more money. But as soon as a player is told by a coach, as I have been many times, that 'here's my theory' or 'that was what I told you' I think the relationship is over, and unlikely to recover.

I told you about the two biggest coaching influences earlier. Coach 1, who I have known for the best part of 30 years, and Coach 2, who came into my life relatively late on and who has extended my career for probably five more years. The season after I started working with him was the most productive of my career. I felt like I was going to perform whatever the format or circumstances every time I played. These guys have no ego whatsoever, but they are pretty rare among coaches.

Luck plays a part, too. I am fortunate to have had those two strong relationships with coaches. A lot of players don't have the luxury of forming such a bond with one coach, never mind two. These days, coaches move counties a lot. It's not quite like football where the average coach or manager lasts 14 months, but it's starting to get that way. I know a lot of pros who have continued to work with their old coach long after he has moved on, sometimes to the detriment of his relationship with his replacement or even without his knowledge. I look at the coaches I still speak to regularly; why would I speak to them after years of not working together? Easy, we built a relationship of trust and care which lasts a lifetime. But if it works for you, why change it? It's your career that's on the line after all. Enlightened coaches accept that, because they recognise it benefits the most important person in the player-coach relationship. The player.

Don't try and coach an old dog new tricks

The longer you play professionally the easier it gets. What I mean by that is eventually you reach a stage in your career when you are comfortable with your technique. You might tweak it now and again, but you trust it. You have grooved it over many years. You start getting somewhere. Longer contracts, better salary perhaps, and eventually international recognition if you can ally your ability with consistency and a strong mentality.

I played at a very high level. It was nice to be recognised, to feel you were on the next rung of the ladder even if, in the back of your mind, you probably accepted as I did that this might be as good as it got. At least this brief taste of life at the (near) top would give you access to good facilities and, you thought, good coaches. Wrong.

Before my first game for an England representative side I worked with an outstanding former player who was one of my first heroes when I was growing up. After three balls of our first session together he walked down the net and told me I couldn't play my way, I had to change. Bear in mind, I'd been a professional for a long time.

Surprise, surprise, the technical change he suggested ruined me for the next few months and I hardly made a run. My point is that in those circumstances any coach should recognise two things: you have reached that point in your career because you have a technique that works for you, even if it might not look aesthetically pleasing, and, secondly, there's no point fixing something which isn't broken. Good coaches adapt to the player rather than try to change him into what they want. In hindsight, I should have pushed back. This guy was a brilliant player, but not in my opinion a good coach at that time.

Now, he probably felt that in the limited time he had to work with us he had to make an impression. Thinking about it, I wondered whether at elite level or just below technical coaches were of any use. After all, as a player you have got that far because your technique has enabled you to produce consistent performances – loads of runs or lots of wickets. You will soon know whether it is good enough to cope with playing against the very best players. At this level it's more important to be a mentor or guide than make wholesale changes in a short period of time.

If it is, great – you've cracked it. If not you will realise, as I did, that no amount of exposure to coaches supposedly regarded as the best in the country because they work with the best players, will make any difference.

It's one of the reasons why I admire players who reach the very top such as Ben Stokes and Jos Buttler. As they travel from country to country, changing formats and teams or franchises on a regular basis, it must be nigh on impossible to build a solid relationship with any of the coaches employed by the teams they play for, simply because of the transitory nature of what they do. It's why a lot of highly paid coaches in the IPL, for instance, are former internationals, employed for their experience of cricket at the very highest level where their mentoring and man-management are more important than pure coaching ability. Coaches can help, but they can't bat or bowl for you.

The Secret Coach

In the past couple of years, I have done some junior coaching. I try to take what I have experienced as a player and go from there when I work with youngsters. For instance, after saying hello I will let the player dictate the conversation. If all they want me to do is turn on the bowling machine and load balls for an hour while they bat then that's fine. As the relationship grows, the player might ask about specific shots or how to deal with different types of bowling. But I like the player to make the first move, not me.

Parents will sometimes ask me if they think their kid could become a professional. Notwithstanding the fact that until he or she is about 15 it's very hard to make that sort of assessment, I try to avoid answering that question because I've seen so many coaches respond in glowing terms about a young player who turns out to be nowhere near good enough. It will then be the coach's fault for raising false hopes, according to parents. Some coaches will take that on the chin because they would rather be criticised than see any disappointment felt by their parents directed at the child instead.

I hear so often about a 'genius' who is 15, or a 12-year-old 'who will make it' that I am fairly immune to it now, but one thing I do know is that so much happens between the ages of 15 to 18 that the player will need a good mentor to guide them through the twists and turns that await. I still speak to mine. Our friendship comes from building trust and isn't just about cricket. The more a coach can look at the person rather than the player their chances of being truly exceptional increase. One of my coaches couldn't always help me with everything technically, but he would be the first to send me a message telling me how important I was to his team and he always made me feel better about myself. These are the types of coaches who you go back to time and again; they care for your career and your success, but ultimately about you as a person.

8

Leadership

FAR GREATER minds than mine have theorised about what makes success in team sport. How do you create the dynamic that brings trophies, glory and a nice bonus? What other factors are at work apart from the skill level of the players?

I've been a part of some very successful teams. I'm lucky to have won plenty of domestic honours and I have played with some extraordinarily talented players, whose performances led us to those successes. But I have also been on rudderless ships and in squads when everything seemed to be in place to be successful, but it has ended up being a disaster.

I don't claim to know all the answers, but this is a topic I have probably spoken about with team-mates and coaches more than any other. After all, everyone wants to be successful at what they do, don't they?

So, based on those discussions (I took notes, you know) here are my thoughts on leaders, leadership and the hierarchy in a county cricket club; what works, what doesn't and what happens when it goes wrong.

Who's in charge?

Is it the coach or the captain? Or can it be both?

The key to making a success of this relationship, which is the most important in any cricket team, is defining those respective roles very early on and sticking to them.

The captain should always have the final say on selection – he has got to have total belief in the ten players who follow him out on to the field. The coach and the captain don't need to have similar personalities, although they have to share similar values and ethics. They can be two of the quietest and most undemonstrative people in the dressing-room, as long as they know their roles and so do the players. In one of the teams I played in that won trophies, if you'd asked someone to observe us for an hour the last person he'd have chosen as the leader would have been the quiet, contemplative guy sitting in the corner fiddling with his bat.

Players are simple folk. We've got enough to worry about trying to stay fit and in the team. For us it always works best when we know who picks the team (captain) and who runs the cricket (coach). The best partnerships would butt heads all the time, and there's nothing at all wrong with that, but the captain always took the team out that he wanted and it was up to the captain and coach to decide who told you if you were dropped and the reasons why. I saw it done in different ways. Sometimes the coach would tell the player he isn't playing but ask them to speak to the captain after the game. It is so important that the captain can focus on their own game as well and not have to deal with a pissed-off player until the match is done and dusted.

If the relationship between the captain and coach is strong and they are in sync there is no need for management groups or senior player think-tanks, which in my experience are time-wasting exercises mostly spent talking about decisions that the coach and captain should be making between themselves.

That sort of consultation among a team should happen organically, whether it's an inquest after a bad defeat or a discussion on how to try and improve collectively. Good coaches and captains should be able to identify leaders among their players and feel able to consult them without the need to form groups, which can create issues for team morale, especially if you are a senior player and don't get invited to these little conclaves. I have seen important players not included in these groups and get thoroughly pissed off over something that really isn't that important. It also adds another meeting to a game already full of pointless meetings. If communication and feedback is consistent and effective, who needs to sit in an office with a flipchart writing down big words which mean absolutely fuck all when the shit hits the fan out in the middle.

What makes a good captain?

The best captains are very rarely the best player or the longest serving, but a lot of counties choose their leaders based on that criteria. I have experienced both and they rarely work out.

There are different types of leaders, and that applies to cricket as much as the boardroom of a conglomerate in the City. Again, the message from us players is clear enough. All we really want to know is what they expect from you.

During the most successful period of my career, when I was helping the team win trophies, the relationship with my captain didn't get any better because we were successful, although it was by no means bad. We got along really well. To be honest, I didn't always agree with him, but I did trust his decision-making on a cricket field. We played in his style which was great for young players to follow as an example. This is vital. You don't always have to agree but knowing it is being done for the good of the team means you will commit fully to the team and its leader.

But even if a captain's gung-ho approach doesn't stir your competitive juices, you can still play under that sort of leader. You don't have to follow it, but if you're smart you will acknowledge that it is good for your career if it brings success.

I'll give you a modern example of a good captain. Look at Somerset. They picked Tom Abell, who was probably not in their top five best players when they appointed him, but is someone who embodied the characteristics and the way they wanted the team to play. The captain leads that, not the coach. When I played against him, he struck me as being quite a cerebral captain.

After we'd beaten them in a Championship game I asked one of his team-mates what he was like. 'He seems to be born to do it,' was the response. 'You can tell he's thinking about the game all the time and he actually seems to be enjoying it. He never gets stressed, even when we are doing badly.' Of course, that approach can lead to accusations that he is too laid back. But it seems to me that he's got it right and you can very clearly see his identity and ethos running throughout the club. To me, this was a clever appointment made with a vision for a club in mind when so many decision-makers make a short-term call to keep their jobs secure. In the case of Somerset, they are in a good position to have sustainable success with a strong culture for the players to buy into, led by the captain.

I have done the job occasionally and I enjoyed making decisions knowing they had no implications for me further than the match we were playing. It's a great feeling to lead a winning team, one of the best experiences of my career.

Captaining every now and then can be good fun, you go unnoticed and you can have an impact in freshening up the team. The hardest thing is when you get given a team to lead at short notice which you have had no input over, no time to mould it to how you would like it to be run, and you are judged very quickly. Being made captain is an extremely prestigious achievement and any leader needs to be able to make key decisions before being told he's rubbish.

A captain deserves at least two years to see if he's suitable, even if results aren't great. That's enough time to assess what he's got, come up with a strategy (along with the coach), and hopefully build a legacy. Any less time than that and you might as well put the names into a hat and pull one out.

What do you think?

Feedback is an area where the game has changed a lot. Until about ten years ago the skipper would always consult his vice-captain and a couple of senior players on major decisions. But these days, especially in one-day cricket, he will just as likely talk to a younger player, especially if they have experience of franchise cricket and can offer suggestions about players and different tactics they have come across. So many players take part in different competitions all over the world these days and it's stupid not to tap into their experiences and knowledge, whether they are 22 or 32.

As a young player, I felt I had achieved something in my career for the first time when I believed I could offer my opinions – a good season, Lions recognition, being awarded your cap. In good teams everyone is encouraged to say something, but in bad teams most players, especially youngsters, tend to keep their mouths shut.

Spreading the load

The days when one player led his team in all three competitions have all but disappeared. Split captaincies can work and it obviously makes sense to employ an experienced white-ball cricketer, or overseas player, to lead your one-day side.

But it can also create issues when one captain is leading a team of superstars who are in contention for trophies while another has got a shitty side and the club has effectively been split into red- and white-ball squads. Being captain of a county in the Championship while not being involved in the white-ball teams is becoming more and more prevalent.

At one of my counties, our white-ball captain was a much stronger character and demanded complete ownership of his team. The coach, who had effectively run the red-ball team because his captain in that format was so inexperienced, found himself compromised to a certain extent. But he let it happen. Good coaches do that because they understand their role and know when to take a step back.

Losing the dressing-room

This is a phrase you often hear in football, just before a manager gets the sack. You might think it happens quite often in cricket because of the time we spend together as a collective, but it is rarely the reason why a coach loses his job. More often it is because he gets a better job. Sometimes the results are terrible or he has lost the trust of his players, but it seldom happens during the season.

When good coaches adapt to the team and its needs, there is harmony. They get to know the players before they start to formulate an identity for that team.

If they tell players what to do, they don't own the team or the dressing-room culture and the relationship is only going one way. The same way as the fortunes of the club who have employed him.

I'm lucky. During my career I experienced some fantastic coaches, but also some poor ones. A new coach walks in and in his first meeting he tells everyone how things are going to be under the new regime, normally in the form of a well-rehearsed PowerPoint presentation, and generally done in a 'me' and 'you' manner. This doesn't work. Players may buy in for a short period, but they then realise that it isn't what the team needs. The short-term kick might work but in my experience the best coaches give players ownership of the team values. If you've got a team who like to be social and ban drinking it is only going to have the opposite effect to that you intended and vice-versa.

The next thing is that the team doesn't do well and a new coach comes in. 'You must get fitter!' he says. Fuck me, yes, that's the answer. We keep getting bowled out for 100 so we need to spend our time lifting weights and being sick running up hills. Every team should be fit enough to do their job. The good coaches make fitness an expectation, and then look at how to make the cricket better. I guess it is easier to look at a sheet of results and pat yourself on the back because a player has improved his bleep test score rather than make that individual more skilful. Not for one minute am I suggesting fitness isn't one the fundamental keys to success – as professional athletes we should all be fit enough to execute our skills day after day. The danger is when you reward fitness over performance, and this doesn't help anyone as we all know runs and wickets win trophies, not bleep test results.

Where this approach can become an absolute shit show it when the new coach comes in and suddenly everyone is in every day doing obscene amounts of 'My way or the highway' fitness sessions and the whole squad, and especially the older players, end up on the physio's table and cannot bowl in April because they have a stress fracture.

Look at Essex for an example of a team with a good identity. They have some fine players, but they are also a very social team, they spend time together away from cricket and build interpersonal relationships that way. That is their identity, and no one can argue that it's not working for them. Somerset pride themselves on how fit they are. That's their identity and works for them, but try to change that overnight and it won't work. I really respect the coaches and captains of teams like this, they are able to give control and ownership to others rather than be scared that they can't oversee every small part and micro-manage the players.

A coach who does not find an identity to fit the group of players he is working with won't last long. The dynamic of the team is unique to those individual players. And if you get it wrong, it is very hard to get back.

In my experience players on the county circuit tend to moan more about their coaches than their team-mates. Hearing opponents eulogise their coach is pretty rare. Coaches such as Matt Walker, Mark Robinson, Kevin Sharp, Richard Dawson and Peter Moores are very highly regarded, and of the more recent recruits to the role so is Anthony McGrath. He has done a fine job at Essex by bringing the team together in a skilled and unique way. Having seen the way Essex operate it is obvious they enjoy doing a few things: playing, winning, spending time together and enjoying themselves and McGrath encourages all of that while developing them as players.

When it does go wrong, though, wow it's bad. The couple of years I played under a bad coach were not enjoyable at all, even though my own form was OK. After the first year I was anticipating a reset, but on our first day back out came the PowerPoint slides again. The slides were in a different order, but the message was the same: 'It's my way'.

We adopted a siege mentality. Everyone was so fed up that moaning about the coach actually strengthened the bond between the players. There were no cliques, because no one supported the coach and everyone was miserable. People outside the dressing-room who worked for the club knew something wasn't right, but when things started to go wrong most people simply looked out for themselves. There was no unity at all. Appeals to the CEO fell on deaf ears.

When it gets that toxic, players who are not scoring runs or taking wickets will tend to blame the bad atmosphere – in other words the coach – for their poor performances, especially if the majority view among the squad is that he is not up to the job. It can get very grim but – and this may surprise you given the amount of time we spend in each other's pockets – physical confrontations are extremely rare. I have never seen team-mates come to blows or heard about it at other counties. Plenty of posturing, shouting and swearing goes on of course, but no punches are thrown. Unlike some footballers, we know how to behave, even when the sky seems to be falling in on our own little world.

Knowing when to stop

Even the most successful coaches, like players, have a shelf life. I would contend that any coach, no matter how many trophies he's helped to win, should think about his future after four years with one club. Either he should move on or he should change the team over a period of time to keep it and him fresh and evolving.

The reality is somewhat different. Trevor Bayliss was pretty clear that he would stay in the England job for four to five years and then move on. That is rare in cricket, but he understood that in elite sport or business things can go stagnant, even when you are successful. Peter Moores has been successful because he's always sought a fresh challenge. He's a fine coach, and he's won trophies at Sussex, Lancashire and Nottinghamshire. I am very impressed with how James Foster is building his career in coaching. He pops up at all sorts of franchise teams and has now started working with England's wicketkeepers. He wants to develop, even if he might have to pay for himself so he can experience different cricket environments and soak up knowledge.

Coaches that stay too long and keep coming out with the same messages eventually become a shadow of themselves. The stuff that used to be positive and fun becomes boring after a couple of years. And if you are doing the same stuff in year three or four as you did in year one you really are in trouble, no matter how successful you have been. Coaches that can shock and surprise you are worth their weight in gold.

I remember one season when we were in a really rough patch in the Championship with a couple of games to go. We were mentally tired because fighting for every point can be draining and we feared for our futures, because we knew there would be a clear-out and three or four players would leave at the end of the season if we went down. But instead of heading to the nets, we all went for coffee, talked to each other in a different environment for a couple of hours … and won our next game. It's a very basic example, but it worked. The best coaches will sometimes give you a day off when every instinct might be to train harder and this can only be done when a coach is thinking clearly and not in a state of fear or emotional turmoil.

Coaching is a vocation that interests me as I think about life after cricket. But there are only 18 first-class counties, so jobs are limited. It is a tough gig and coaching staffs will get shit when the team lose, but rarely much credit when they win. Assistant coaches work so hard and don't always get the pay or credit they deserve. I have seen some great assistants become stagnant after too long without getting a shot at the top job and lose their passion, as well as experiencing knee and shoulder problems from endless hours in the nets. As in a whole host of professions, you need people to see you in a new light from time to time and in county cricket jobs can sometimes become just that, a job. For me the only job in any cricket team that should be held for any length of time is the scorer.

But I would say this. County coaching is a 12-month-a-year occupation. I don't think it can be done properly if you are only with the players for pre-season and the summer months. That's especially important in these straitened times when Brexit and the financial effects of the global pandemic have left clubs increasingly reliant on bringing through their own players. You can't properly monitor player development if you're only there from March to September, which makes me question some of the high-profile overseas appointments we have seen in the county game over the years.

Who's accountable?

County cricket thinks of itself as an elite sporting environment, but still employs a lot of people, often in decision-making positions, who don't seem to be accountable and appear to have a job for life. I think it's one of the biggest issues in the game.

In football, managers get the sack all the time, but when a head coach loses his job at a county cricket club it's a shock. I remember reading about Jim Troughton getting the chop from Warwickshire at the end of the 2020 season. I don't know the ins and outs of what went on there, although it's fair to say they haven't made much progress in the past few years and expectations are high at a big club like

Warwickshire. But I was still shocked to hear that he'd been fired.

Look around county cricket. Some members of the 'clite' structure have been in post for years. But do you, as a fan of a particular county, know what their role actually entails and to whom he or she is accountable? I can count on one hand the number of serious cricketing conversations I had with the person who was my line manager at one of the counties I played for. We never saw him in the dressing-room or in the nets. Quite a few of the younger players in the squad didn't know who he was, far less what he did.

He never fronted up in the media when things were going badly, leaving that job to the captain and coach. If I wanted to know something or talk about my next contract I used to by-pass him and go straight to the chief executive. I didn't trust his judgement and neither did most of my team-mates.

I have also experienced some really good managers, who are on top of their brief, who know who the best player in the under-11s is as well as how many wickets their leading bowler took last season. You don't have to have played the game at a high level to be good at the job either. Someone like Alec

Stewart at Surrey has a strong profile in the game and he might be able to persuade world-class players to join him. But Andy Hurry at Somerset has a military background with a lot of strategic and planning experience, and he has done a brilliant job with them. It isn't a one-size-fits-all strategy, but these are huge roles, generally well paid, and I think the clubs who are creating successful squads also have trusted individuals with clearly defined roles in the important positions.

Cricket certainly needs more people from outside cricket to shake things up a bit. In terms of structure, county clubs are probably 25 years behind Premier League football, whose organisations tend to be ruthless when it comes to hiring and firing. When things don't work out in cricket the answer tends to be a reshuffle and restructure, not fundamental change.

9

Hiring, Firing, Earning, Recruiting and Moving

COUNTY CRICKETERS are generally content with their lot. Most of us don't earn the money that is available in other sports like football and rugby unless we reach the very top, and even then the sums world-class cricketers earn are still nowhere near those at the top of their profession in other sports.

But it's still a nice life. You're comfortably off, you can afford a nice place to live, a decent car and a couple of holidays a year. If you've got your head screwed on, and in my experience most players have, you'll also be putting money away for when your career ends and the taps are turned off, which can happen without warning if you get, say, a career-ending injury.

Unlike some football clubs, county cricket clubs don't go bust with 25 players suddenly finding themselves unemployed. They are stable institutions and in some cases have been for hundreds of years. You get paid on time; you get your bonus when it's due; there's always a nice car for you to drive at the start of the season. You have a lot to be thankful for, which is why most players stay with the same county throughout their careers, even if it lasts ten years or longer.

I thought I'd be the same, but I opted for a change of scene. I was still performing consistently in red- and white-ball formats; I was one of the best-paid players in our dressing-room; I was settled and, from the outside, I probably looked pretty happy with my lot. I had won trophies, which a lot of players never manage. But when I sat down with my wife one day and had a serious think about what I wanted to do with the next few years of my career I concluded that I couldn't spend it where I was, even though there were more practical reasons to stay than to move.

I wasn't playing for a bad club, but it had become a badly-run club. This is usually what makes players leave.

The majority of county pros do not play for counties who win trophies on a regular basis. Some can have a 15–20 year career and never win anything, but they are perfectly content because they know there is a plan, a strategy, an identity, joined-up thinking, something to believe in at their place of work. Here are a couple of examples. At Worcestershire there is a clear structure built around developing young players; Northamptonshire have tended to concentrate on white-ball cricket in recent years and punched above their weight. Counties who commit themselves to a clearly defined strategy might experience some short-term pain but the best ones – Somerset and Essex are other good examples – know that in the long term it will bear fruit.

I took a long look at the 18 counties in 2020 and wondered what the strategy was at some of them. What are they actually trying to achieve and who is either driving things forward and, more importantly, what happens if Plan B doesn't work out? Are Yorkshire a club who still covet the Championship above anything else? Do Lancashire now see themselves as a one-day powerhouse? Are Surrey going the same way?

Anyway, the more I thought about my own situation the more the doubts crept in. We didn't have a strategy and I didn't trust the decision-makers to come up with one any time soon. We were drifting from season to season, there didn't seem to be a plan.

I couldn't work out what the recruitment strategy was or what sort of culture the club was trying to nurture. What were their goals and what was the timescale to achieve them in?

Previously, when my contract had been up for renewal the club had begun negotiating with me 18 months before it was due to expire. A meeting with the director of cricket and chief executive was arranged, but then the D of C spent all of his time negotiating contracts with some of our junior pros – and I heard nothing. I rang one of the players concerned, who I knew, like me, wanted to find out what the club's medium- and long-term goals were. He told me that when he asked that question he was greeted with a blank expression. 'We're just here to talk about next season.'

That got me thinking and a few weeks later, when what was a perfectly reasonable contract offer was finally tabled, I decided to turn it down. By the following April, with my contract running down, I was effectively on the market because this is the earliest in the year a player can be approached by another county. There was a lot of interest once the news was out there. I was quite flattered. But now I was facing the sort of dilemma that most pros never have to worry about as I thought about my options.

There is so much more to consider: how will it affect your family? Where are you going to live? Do you buy somewhere, rent or live in the hotel on the ground? Are you going to win things or have a chance of competing for honours? What is the strategy?

Whatever I decided, I wanted the decision to be made purely for cricketing reasons. I wanted to be able to look back and be at peace with myself. So much so that I turned down a county who were a lot closer to home, which meant I wouldn't have had to uproot the family and who would have paid me more money. They also had a youngish squad, and I guessed if I had done even reasonably well for the length of my contract I would have got an extension and been able to contemplate playing into my 40s. Fortunately, my wife never considered anything else other than my career when we talked things over, even though she knew it would mean spending a lot of time travelling around and compromise on her behalf to make it work.

My decision was based on experience, but for everyone like me there is a pro who moves for an extra £10k to an area of the country where it might be cheaper to live and instantly regrets it. I have played with a few such players over the years and it's not much fun for them or their team-mates. One hadn't even played a game for us when he asked the CEO if he could convert his three-year deal into a one-year contract with a year's option. It's one of the reasons why so many counties are reluctant to publicise the length of a player's contract these days, a bail-out option for both parties. Needless to say he'd left by the end of his first season and ended up back at his old county, but on less money than when he left.

I was happy with my own decision once I considered various factors. From playing against them I knew the players at my new county were, on the whole, pretty good blokes. The ground and facilities were excellent, and I had a lot of respect for the backroom staff. More importantly, when I went to speak to them, they had all the answers when I asked what the plan was, the vision. I showed my commitment by buying a house in the area and focusing on the task at hand.

It's not always as straightforward, of course, and when I moved counties my agent did make the whole process a lot smoother.

Having an agent is not just an ego thing. If you have been at a club for three or four years and are not sure of your financial standing when it comes to your next contract they will generally know what you're worth. Agents constantly speak to counties to find out what sort of players they are looking to recruit. Good clubs will be planning two or three years ahead. The agent will know who is out of contract and when and can put pieces of the jigsaw into place.

When I first used an agent I was earning £35k a year. The club offered me £45k. I gave the agent 20% of every £1k he got me above that figure, and he got me another £5k. Happy days. A few years later I wanted £70k but took £60k with a bonus structure that ended up earning me £90k. I found bonus structures to be a great way to earn a bit more than perhaps you should, and with a clever agent it became a game of smoke and mirrors. Again, that was down to him being on top of his game.

Watching them at work with directors of cricket is very instructive. Most of these guys know very little about tax, national insurance or PAYE. A good agent can use that lack of fiscal nous and tie a D of C in knots and earn their client a few more grand. This happened on a couple of occasions, before the CEO discovered what was going on and insisted on conducting negotiations with senior players (and their agents) himself. That was fine by me, because these guys are usually the ones who know exactly how much money there is in the pot.

This may sound like I was out to take the piss but the thing to always remember is that a professional athlete will start training when they are 10–12 and commit their lives to the profession and sacrifice a huge amount to reach this stage. A career is generally short in cricket, and although you may earn £50–90k for a few years, if you get injured or have a lean time you are quickly discarded and then what are you left with? Very few qualifications and no job experience in the real world.

Agents generally charge 5% commission. Some are former players, others work in football and rugby. Well-connected agents can get you franchise contracts. I know some agents have a bad reputation in football, but in my experience the guys that work in cricket are pretty good. Often they love the game, which helps.

I did my own contract negotiations in the early years of my career because I knew I wouldn't be getting massive pay increases. When I see 19-year-olds earning £20k a year with an agent I do laugh. I only hope that in those circumstances the agents aren't charging a fee, in the expectation that the player continues to use their services when he goes up the pay scale.

In the second half of my career, I cared more about the bonuses in my contract than the basic salary. By incentivising your contract more, you can be very well rewarded for simply producing consistent performances. You always compare your runs and wickets to players of equivalent stature in your team and if they earned more than you – because remember everyone in the dressing-room knows roughly what everyone else is earning – it's a good way of getting a few more grand on your next deal.

Cricket offers a good salary when you have played for a long time as I did, but the more you earn the more vulnerable you are. If you're on £80–120k and have two bad years in your mid- to late-30s the chances are you're gone, whereas if you are in your mid-20s and have two bad years but you're earning £35k the likelihood is you will be kept on.

Once you have been playing for ten years you should be on good money, minimum £70k a year with a good bonus structure. By then you are in the top 100 in your profession. The trouble is that at some time between the ages of 30 and 40 that is likely to end. You have dedicated 25 years of your life to cricket, got kids, a nice house with a mortgage paid for on the strength of that salary and had a great time, but then you look at your contemporaries working in the financial sector earning £120k with no time limit on their careers. That is a massive reality check. Unless you are in the very top bracket, the 5% who play for England and have an IPL contract, you are going to have to work for a long time after you stop playing. That's the scary part – when it all stops.

Sometimes it can get so bad at a county that you leave before your contract expires, the old 'mutual consent' which you quite often see in football. It happens much less frequently in cricket, but it can be very difficult to extricate yourself from a contract if the county are keen to keep you to it. There have been instances in the past where players have had to pay a nominal sum to terminate their contract early, but this is rare in the county game. Most players prefer to keep their money in their pocket.

I wonder if at some stage in the future cricket will, like football, have a transfer system where freedom of movement is made easier. I certainly think counties should be compensated when a player that they have developed from an early age, say 15 years onwards, moves on when their contract expires. You won't stop players moving to bigger counties for more money or so they have a better opportunity of winning trophies and being successful, but the 'buying' county might think twice if they have to pay a transfer fee to his county as well as a fat contract. It might force them to consider their strategies and invest more into their development of players. And it at least gives the county who have lost one of their assets the financial clout to help replace him.

You don't want a situation in cricket which you see at some football clubs who have abandoned youth development altogether, but what is the point in investing in an academy system and a pathway if you are not compensated when a player you have developed moves on?

Or what about some sort of draft system? Many counties have started to trim their squads because of the financial repercussions of COVID. So how about each county having 18 players plus two international players and then a draft to choose up to four more from those who are out of contract and looking for a new county. I don't think any idea which makes county cricket leaner and more adaptable should be ignored. It would certainly make a lot of them more streamlined and place greater emphasis on the make-up of the playing squad.

One area where I think cricket lags behind other sports like football and rugby is the recruitment of players. Existing players, their agents, directors of cricket, members of the coaching staff, chief executives, committee members – they all play their part, but there has always seemed to me to be a lack of structure. At some counties the head coach will have the final say. At others he will recommend players and ask his superiors to get on with it.

The best people to talk to about potential signings are us, the players. We talk all the time, to team-mates and players at other clubs, on the circuit. We know what is going on and with players frequently spending winters abroad we are usually aware about a potential Kolpak signing or can find out a bit more about him.

Not so long ago there was no formal procedure when it came to approaching a player. We were tapped up all the time. I remember it happening to me a couple of times when I was batting and the wicketkeeper and slip, who was also captain, asked about my contract situation and whether I fancied a change of scene. The end-of-season PCA awards always used to be a great place to find out which players were out of contract and available. Agents are always useful, but there are still a few senior players who don't have them and prefer to negotiate their own contracts or moves to another county.

Just as long as it's not left to committee or board members. I remember a few years ago, when I'd just got established in the side and was now regarded as a senior figure in the dressing-room, and one of our committee men sidled up to me after play. 'I'm just about to go into the committee meeting and I'd like to let you know that I'm going to recommend we sign Virat Kohli, because he seems to get an awful lot of runs for India. Anyway, I thought I'd tell you that if we do get him he's potentially going to take your position.

'It's all in here,' he added, pointing to a ring-binder which had two pieces of A4 inside and a label on the front with 'Koli' on it. He couldn't even spell his name right!

Needless to say, this global icon didn't come anywhere near our county, but I was told later that there was a serious debate about this proposal until the head coach, who had turned up late to the meeting to present his monthly report, heard about the Kohli plan and told the committee that their idea was laughable; how would we have found £300k to pay for him when we could barely afford to feed the players in pre-season!

Football clubs, and not just in the Premier League, have their own recruitment departments these days and I've always thought cricket clubs who had a specialist in this field could save their counties a fortune. Money is tight and will become even tighter in the post-COVID and Brexit world so getting the right players in at the right price, and then making sure they are settled and able to perform, seems to me to be absolutely crucial.

But our game is littered with stories of players signed on two-, three- or even four-year contracts on improved money who then struggle. I'm convinced that it is often down to a lack of detailed research before the player is signed. What's his record like at his new home ground? Have there been any issues on the field with any of his new team-mates? What are his family's priorities in terms of schooling for his kids? Will the area suit him? Can he afford to buy a property and, if not, what does he need in terms of a rented place? Is English his first language and, if not, what provision should we make to get over that? What about his partner and his or her needs? All these and many other questions need to be asked but from what I have experienced throughout my career they don't always get answered.

And remember, it's not just the player himself who suffers if he can't score the runs or take the wickets he was brought in to produce. It has an effect on the rest of us because it reduces our chances of winning trophies.

Recruitment changed markedly when the UK left the European Union in 2020. There are no Kolpaks, they are now classified as overseas players. Overall, my experience of Kolpaks is that they have definitely improved the standard of our domestic cricket. Most are incredibly driven to succeed because they regard this as the best opportunity in their careers to make some decent money for them and their families, particularly the guys who come over from South Africa where the rand is very weak compared to sterling.

It's a short career, you've got to cash in when you can. Even those not in the top bracket of players back home had a lot of talent, trained hard and were fiercely competitive on the pitch. I enjoyed playing alongside them because I felt they helped me to get better as well because I didn't want to be compared badly to anyone.

There is an argument that they prevented English-qualified players from getting opportunities, and early in my career I would have sympathised with that view. At my first county we had two overseas players and a Kolpak so it was difficult for me to get into the team. I never complained to the coach and captain because I didn't think it was their fault that I wasn't considered good enough at that stage. I had to get better, initially by doing well in the second team, and that's what happened. There are still eight places in the team available. Good players will always find a way in.

The same characteristics which I think Kolpaks brought to our game apply to overseas players in general. I can count on one hand the number I played against or with over the past 20 years who didn't cut it. They generally have a great attitude, they work and train hard and they are happy to pass on their experiences from playing in other parts of the world.

I'm not sure overseas players have a massive respect for the English game, but they do leave with a lot of respect for our players who find playing in English conditions really challenges them. They appreciate how hard it can be to score runs in the top four, where most of them bat, on seaming English wickets. And for bowlers, they realise how hard English pros work when there is precious little time for rest and recovery. Even ten years ago most recognised that if they could get through April and May they might cash in when surfaces improved from June onwards.

The thing they do moan about is the schedule; they can't understand why we play so much. In that regard they are mostly preaching to the converted.

Who can blame your overseas bowler for going through the motions on the fourth afternoon of a Championship match on a dead pitch if the game is going nowhere? If it were me, I know I would.

Batting in the top six against some of these guys was a proper battle. With a new ball and fresh pitch to bowl on, they never dropped down a gear. It used to make me laugh when our No.7 and 8 would come back in after whacking the opposition's overseas bowler around a bit late in the day and tell us all how easy it was. To which I would reply something along the lines of, 'Try fucking facing him half an hour into the day, when he's into his third or fourth over and finding a nice rhythm.' There might have been a couple more f-words.

I have played against some of the best players in the world, guys like Muttiah Muralitharan, Shane Warne, V.V.S. Laxman to name but a few. If you couldn't get motivated against top players like those, what is the point in playing?

As I say, most were fantastic, but I remember once when our county signed an overseas all-rounder who performed on the pitch but was a complete prick off it. During his spell with us I effectively ended up being his chaperone. So much so that I had to go in advance to check that his hotel room was up to standard before he even set foot in it. Honestly, he used to turn his nose up at a Corby trouser press! The club put him up in a hotel near the ground when he arrived and within a couple of hours he'd walked out because it wasn't a five-star establishment. I was just leaving the ground after practice when our CEO, who was looking a bit flustered, buttonholed me in the car park.

The upshot was I had to go to his hotel, load all his gear into my car and drive him to the only five-star place in town where, needless to say, he was happy only when he'd settled into its only suite. An exception to the rule, but the sort of hassle that could have been avoided if we'd done our research on him properly.

In my experience even the guys who come from overseas and end up playing for several counties put everything in everywhere they go. Their personal standards won't allow them to coast. A good example is Ross Taylor, the former New Zealand captain. He played for four or five counties, but every time you played against him his team-mates were always very complimentary about his willingness to embrace that team and its own beliefs.

I certainly noticed their absence in 2020 when, because of the pandemic, only two or three overseas players made it over, and then just to play in the Blast. The drop in the overall standard in the Bob Willis Trophy, the four-day competition which replaced the Championship, was very noticeable. I'm all for young players getting an opportunity and the circumstances were extraordinary, but I also strongly believe that elite sport should be elite – the best against the best. When I saw some of the youngsters getting first-class matches who had barely played any second-team cricket it pissed me off a bit, because I remember how hard I had to work for that chance. It is something that must be earned and it will be better for them in the long run.

Apart from your salary and any sponsorships, the only other way of making a big lump sum during your career is a benefit or testimonial.

If you can clear £50k from your benefit these days – and remember it is still tax free up to a certain figure, although whether that remains the case for much longer is doubtful – then you have done well.

I think the benefit system will disappear in five years, perhaps less. I certainly feel sorry for guys who were awarded one in 2020 or have one coming to them over the next couple of years. The implications of the pandemic on the business world are going to be huge. If you are lucky you got your benefit at a time of relative economic prosperity when companies weren't looking to cut expendable stuff like sponsorship.

You could have been a world-class player for your county and have had yours in 2009 after the financial crash when companies cut back on sponsorship. Then you might have watched an average county player smash five times your amount two years later purely because the economic landscape in 2011 was better. During tough times I have seen dinners being cancelled, freebies dished out and great auction prizes being bought for next to nothing. Then two years later the same prizes go for ten times that amount.

You also need to have a good organiser. The days when county pros used to have an event a week, even if that 'event' was visiting a pub and opening a massive bottle full of coins for him to take home, disappeared a long time ago. The emphasis in recent years has been on quantity not quality. Six well-organised and, more importantly, well-attended events can get you close to that six-figure sum. To have a successful benefit and sell out the big events is becoming rare, but is a great buzz.

I reckon there are probably six or seven counties where with a bit of luck you can make £60k, or even a bit more. It must be so much more difficult for players at smaller clubs in certain parts of the country. I know of internationals who have played for so-called smaller counties having to cancel events or organise things for free like champagne tasting just to create interest, and still make next to nothing.

Whoever you are, the maths are still tight. A decent MC to host the event will charge £1k, a comedian who has been on TV up to £5k. Ex-pros with a profile will cost anything up to £2k so you have to shift a decent number of tickets straight away before you start making any money.

I was lucky to play for a well-supported club so when events were scheduled they sold and we managed to have successful auctions. Luckily, we also had some great people behind the scenes who gave a lot of time, effort and money to help and it was much appreciated and certainly made benefits successful at our club.

I can't explain why a signed bat from a county can fetch £25 one day and then £600 two weeks later, but it just goes that way. The right crowd, plenty of booze and a good atmosphere can lift an auction from awkward to amazing. I have seen average prizes go for thousands once a couple of wealthy business types start competing, and on the flip side unbelievable prizes struggle to make a couple of hundred quid at the wrong event. I've seen prizes I thought would go for a couple of thousand, scrape £200. The couple who bought it couldn't believe their luck and promptly had the night of their lives for nothing, but that's the nature of the beast and it can be amazing, frustrating, embarrassing and exhilarating all at the same time.

There is nothing ethical about a benefit. It's about making as much money as you can to help you move out of the game. I reckon at most events the beneficiary probably knows about 20% of the people in the room personally. You would see a lot of the same people in attendance, including quite a few reluctant team-mates. I never understood that. I always supported benefit events for others, not least because I knew it was an opportunity to cultivate contacts when my own turn at the trough came along.

What I found a bit disingenuous were team-mates who would never make the effort during the season to pop over to the sponsors' boxes during a game for a drink and a bit of small talk. Then, when their benefit came along, you couldn't keep them out of the place. Sponsors aren't daft. They tend to be successful in their businesses and they can spot bullshitters a mile off.

In my experience, if a player asks the guys in the England dressing-room to turn up to an event or provide a decent auction prize they will always help out. Sometimes they won't respond to a text or email, but they probably get asked so many times and not just from team-mates or fellow pros. If you tell a table of sponsors they are going to be sitting with a superstar it doesn't mean you can charge more for the ticket, but when it comes to the auction they tend to dig a bit deeper into their pockets.

Sometimes it can go embarrassingly wrong. We were playing at Lord's one year and the opposition's beneficiary had arranged a dinner in the Long Room with 'the touring New Zealand team'. Unfortunately for him, his organiser hadn't actually invited the touring New Zealand team and it was only on the morning of the event that the player found out. Somehow, he managed to persuade a couple of the coaches and backroom staff to attend but guests who had paid £75 a ticket were not amused. When it came to the auction, his star item – a bat signed by the 2005 England Ashes-winning team – fetched £60. I think the case it came in cost double that amount.

When I started it wasn't unheard of for the top players to have a benefit and a testimonial, but those were the days before franchise cricket opened so many new opportunities for players to earn more money. I can't believe anyone in the current England set-up will have a county benefit or would even need one. As we recover from the economic effects of the pandemic, more people might think again about giving money to someone who is already earning far more than them.

10

How Lucky Am I?

YOU'VE GOT this far in the book and are wondering where the juicy stuff is like racism, ball tampering or match fixing. Well, here we go, but I'm going to have to disappoint you. From my experience of the past 20 years or so I don't think county cricket has a major problems with these issues, and I day this from my day-to-day experiences.

As cricketers we are all guilty of being too wrapped up in our own game most of the time, but when we get the opportunity I think English professionals do appreciate the experiences that being in an environment with people from so many different countries and cultures offers them. We get to meet, travel and live with so many different people. We travel the world to places we may never have visited had it not been that we play cricket for a living. It also gives us the opportunity to immerse ourselves in different cultures and religions in a way most people don't get unless they pay for it on holiday.

A lot has been said in the media on the topic of racism in cricket and sport in general. The allegations made by Azeem Rafiq against Yorkshire in 2020 were appalling, and we all hope that they are investigated thoroughly to prevent it happening again. No one deserves to be treated like he did, and I count myself extremely fortunate not to have witnessed events like this during my career. I have played with so many players from a range of backgrounds and the clubs I have played with were warm and welcoming whilst embracing the differences in our cultures. I consider myself lucky to have had such rewarding experiences in the environments I have been a part of. I did , however, witness an on-field incident which was extremely painful to the player involved, who was a key part of our squad.

The reaction of our club was testament to how we treated players from any background, but we were all unhappy with how it was dealt with by the ECB.

The player concerned got a ban, but the punishment did not fit the crime.

But while incidents of racist behaviour on the field remain blissfully few, that's not to say there isn't an issue with diversity in the English game. Again, based on my experiences from joining an academy set-up to nearly 20 years as a pro, I have only ever worked with one non-white coach, and that was back in my junior days. Now I have probably worked with close to 50 coaches during my career around the world, some for many years and others for just one session. I know the lack of diversity is a big issue for the PCA and ECB which they are trying to address.

The 'Rooney Rule' whereby a certain number of BAME candidates must be interviewed for coaching positions in county cricket has been introduced which is a step forward, but as in football it could be a long time before there are significant numbers of coaches from non-white backgrounds operating in the professional arena, which is still overwhelmingly white and predominantly middle-class. I don't profess to know the answers, but I have played with a lot of black and Asian players who I think would make brilliant coaches; their divergent backgrounds means they often approach things in unconventional and interesting ways. All they need is an opportunity.

I hope it will only take one person from a BAME background to become a successful county coach and others will follow. I haven't worked with Vikram Solanki, who took charge at Surrey in 2020, but speaking to the players there he is very highly regarded. He might be the coach who breaks down those barriers because if cricket is to stay relevant in the 21st century it needs to become more diverse. I think we can all agree on that.

We certainly need to call out people who make racist allegations or slurs a lot more when it has happened away from the field of play. I learnt so much from having team-mates from different backgrounds and most county pros, I think, will say the same. And when we won trophies we all shared in the success, whether we toasted our victories with a bottle of beer or a coke.

Which, admittedly in a clumsy way, brings me to drinking, and what I think has been a massive culture change during the past 15–20 years. When I started we would drink after play nearly every day, especially on away trips. Four or five pints or a bottle of wine, in the hotel or a pub or bar recommended by the opposition, was the norm and those with strong constitutions would really make a night of it. We were young, fit and had a few quid in our pockets. Why wouldn't we?

I remember one away trip early in my career which came during the week when exams finished, and the local student population were letting their hair down. We lost touch with one of our team-mates, who hooked up with a girl in a nightclub and disappeared back to her student accommodation. He turned up the next morning five minutes before the team coach was due to leave, grabbed his bag, napped on the journey to the ground and when he got there, did a ten-minute warm-up before being sick as a dog on the outfield. Then at 11 o'clock he walked out to bat on a green seamer and creamed a brilliant hundred!

Most coaches back then indulged that sort of behaviour, and quite a few could easily keep up with the most thirsty of their players. You would always make a point of socialising with the opposition on at least one night, but then around about 2010 it almost disappeared from the game. If that incident I mentioned had happened ten years later there was a good chance the player concerned would have been snapped at some stage during his all-nighter, the photo posted on social media and he would have got a hefty fine. For a time, players got a bit paranoid about having their photo taken in a social situation for fear of getting accused of anything. I have even seen players turn down selfies with fans because of this paranoia. This is such a shame as most cricket supporters just want a memento of their meeting with a hero. It says a lot for the world we live in.

Thankfully, in the last couple of years, we seem to have found a happy balance. Players don't go out on benders during games, but most counties have made the effort to socialise with the opposition for an hour after at least one day's play. Sitting talking to someone like the umpire Ian Gould for instance taught me more in an hour about the game than weeks of coaching.

Even young players have now realised that there's more to life than protein shakes and spending all your time at the gym, and that having a drink with your mates is mentally very good for you.

I don't think county cricket has got a big drugs problem, because these days the testing regimes are so regular. You can get tested 20–30 times a season and we even get twice-yearly testing for recreational drug use, when they take a sample of your hair (armpit hair for the baldies).

The PCA introduced hair testing a few years back to try to help players if they are spiralling into a wider issue of addiction. The rules are meant to protect the players and enable them to get help if things are taking a turn for the worse. Whilst performance-enhancing drugs are taken to cheat on the field, the use of social drugs indicate that player may be having a tough time, or just made a stupid mistake. What I hope is that players are treated as human beings and the rules are designed to protect the integrity of the game and the welfare of the players. As it stands we have one set of tests to stop you cheating and one to protect you and intervene.

Going back a few years there was the case when one of the most famous players in the world was banned for taking a diuretic to lose weight. Who knows what the real story was there, but if I thought a drug might help me score an extra ten runs per innings or take another two wickets I don't think I would take it. The risk just isn't worth it. We aren't

Olympic athletes where a split second is the difference between glory or failure. Cricket takes sustained skill over a long period of time where a combination of physical and mental strength combined with skill is what gets you to the top, not a drug that helps you run a bit quicker.

Match fixing is potentially a more serious issue for the game. There have been a few games when I've thought something is not quite right and you can see why vulnerable players, who might have financial issues or whose families may have been threatened, can be targeted. It's not for any of us to judge. On the face of it, it would be easy to say to anyone who was caught 'screw you, you're a match fixer' but we don't know the pressure he was under. We all make bad choices. Hearing Mervyn Westfield talk about his experiences, how he came to be in prison, was a lesson for us all that anyone could be affected by this.

We have all sat in dressing-rooms after a game and wondered if something that happened was a bit dodgy. Rumours go round the circuit now and again, but I'm not one to question another player's integrity. Accusing someone of match fixing is saying to them that they committed a crime. People go to prison for match fixing and might get banned for life – it's not the kind of accusation you want to make lightly.

Ball tampering is a funny one. I've played against and with a few teams over the years who had extremely good 'ball management'. I am not accusing anyone of ball tampering; I'll leave that to the men in white coats. I think the best teams manage the ball the best. We get given a ball for 90 overs, so you have to make it work for you and keep it moving. Whether that is keeping one side dry or the spinner getting their hands in the dust or throwing it into the wicket ends, these all take skill to actually create an advantage. The best teams use it to help make them even stronger; it is then skilful bowlers who can use it to take wickets on flat pitches.

It is quite amusing watching teams try and 'manage the ball'. Seeing a team trying to keep the ball dry and then some idiot throwing it on to the green grass or shining it with wet hands always makes me laugh. That is why it is a skill and the best teams do it so well and the crap teams don't have a clue what they are doing.

Similarly, I remember a T20 game when I picked up the ball and it was covered in scratch marks. I threw it to the umpire and said something like, 'What the fuck is that?' The umpire just laughed, and with some justification. The opposition had scored over 200 and we were rattling along at 12 runs an over, so any tampering of the ball was having a negligible effect. At the end of the over he went over to their captain, held the ball up to the light and said, 'Look, if you're going to tamper with the ball at least do it properly.'

11

Around The Grounds

EIGHTEEN COUNTIES and eighteen county grounds, some of them modestly appointed, others stadiums and, in the case of Middlesex, Lord's, the best ground in the world, never mind England.

I've played in them all so here's a snapshot of what they are like. Fellow players who read this will be nodding to themselves, I'm sure. We all have our favourites, and places once visited we would rather not have to go back to again. Sometimes it's because you have a good record there, but more often it's because the food is decent, the hotel you stay at is the best on the circuit or, in the case of quite a few of my county contemporaries, it's where you met your future wife.

Derbyshire

The old pavilion and changing rooms at Derby were pretty horrendous with one toilet between the whole squad. As I mentioned in an earlier chapter, the fantastic food – at least until the sports scientists got involved – more than made up for the fairly dull nature of the ground. And don't get me started on the hotels in Derby. I pray for anyone who stays at the 'inn' overlooking the ground. Once, I got given my room key and unlocked the door to discover it was already occupied by a couple as surprised to see me as I was them.

Durham

In a word, cold, no matter what time of year. No chance of ever getting sunburn at Chester-le-Street. Cold in the sunshine, very cold when it's cloudy. The highlight there was always a proper roast if you were playing on a Sunday but, like three-course feasts at Derby, this has slowly gone as fitness coaches have spread their influence.

Never a nice place to play but generally the game is over quite quickly either way and because it's such a long way for most teams there is usually the prospect of an extra night in Durham, where most teams stay, which is one of the most sociable spots on the circuit.

Essex

Some players don't like Chelmsford, but it has a unique charm. As mentioned, the dressing-rooms are among the hottest environments known to county cricketers but it's got a nice feel to it and the locals are friendly and knowledgeable, although it can get a bit rowdy on T20 nights. Chelmsford is the only ground where you have to share the showers with the opposition and the chance to check out whether the rumours on the circuit about their overseas fast bowler really are true.

Glamorgan

Great city to visit and because Cardiff is the capital of Wales you are generally going to be in a decent hotel. Pitches there are pretty dodgy, though, and it can feel a bit soulless during T20 games as crowds aren't great, but Glamorgan have always been quite a nice bunch of lads to play against.

Gloucestershire

Bristol was quite a bleak place to play county games until they demolished the old grey-bricked children's orphanage with those new flats overlooking the ground. Pitches there can be very attritional, and games can be a bit dull. The changing-rooms aren't the best either, usually freezing and quite dark. It's a cold ground, too. I've worn two jumpers there at least once in every month of the season.

Hampshire

Hampshire have always had a good bunch of lads and the Ageas Bowl is a nice place to play but, as with so many grounds, the changing-rooms are tucked away and never get any sunshine so are always cold. Back in the day the visitors' changing-room had an amazing Jacuzzi, but after a couple of years it got shut down because we used to sit in it for ages after a day's play having a beer and the caretaker wanted to lock up. We stayed there until 11pm once.

Kent

One of the rowdier crowds when you field on the boundary. For a smallish ground you get more shit here from the fans at Canterbury than you would in front of 20,000 at Trent Bridge. Far too many steps up to the changing-rooms, which feel like they are in the attic, but there's a decent view once you get there. Tunbridge Wells is always a nice trip, one of the better outgrounds.

Lancashire

I like Old Trafford. There's a sense of history and it's just over the road from the football ground. If Manchester United are at home you can normally get tickets, even if it's sold out. You are looked after, and the food is good. I do miss getting abused by the members now that the changing-rooms are at the opposite end of the ground though, which makes crowd interaction minimal. There used to be a set of steps you had to walk up in the pavilion that the press called 'The Pit of Hate' because of the stick Lancashire players used to get. It's a shame that when you beat them these days you can't hear the members moaning.

Leicestershire

One of the quirkier grounds. The nets are some of the best on the circuit but are surrounded by barbed wire, the dressing-rooms are tiny, yet Grace Road has one of the biggest outfields there is. You can turn up sometimes and barely see where the wicket is. I have played on some very flat pitches there.

Middlesex

If you get Lord's in the fixtures you celebrate, but it's a lottery with the outgrounds they use. Southgate and Merchant Taylors' School used to be quite pleasant, Uxbridge less so.

London is always a fun away trip and it ends up being a decent week. Get some shopping done on the training day and have a few pints in the Tavern every night. The dressing-room attendants here are world class as are the showers and the toilets are the warmest on the circuit.

Northamptonshire

As mentioned, the County Ground is a good place to lose weight as the food has been awful for years, once bad enough for the whole squad to go down with diarrhoea. Another ground with one toilet in the middle of the dressing-room. Normally a good wicket to play on and the pub at the entrance to the ground is a good place for a post-match pint and the mini M&S in the garage opposite is a life-saver.

Nottinghamshire

Trent Bridge is another cracking away trip. One of the better dressing-rooms (with two attendants), great food and a lovely place to play with a sense of fun, especially on T20 nights. Like a lot of places with a big student population, it's a great city for a night out and for the younger members of the squad there's the opportunity to get a trip to Hooters out of their system.

Surrey

The Oval reminds me a bit of Trent Bridge. Lovely old pavilion and the wickets there are always decent. T20 nights can be really fun, especially if you win. The crowd don't care. Most of them are corporates on a night out getting tanked up who don't support anyone.

A lot closer to central London than Lord's as well, and you never stay in a poor hotel south of the Thames.

Sussex

Always a fun trip to the seaside, and a nice place to play. Most teams stay on the seafront which can be pretty lively most of the year. The old changing-rooms in the pavilion with the big enamel bath weren't the best, but they are now a decent size, and the crowd are always quite friendly to the opposition. Food isn't that great, so the ice-cream van by the deckchairs always gets a visit.

Somerset

Whoever designed the new pavilion didn't consider that big orange thing in the sky. Hottest changing-rooms on the circuit – even hotter than Chelmsford – and designed like a greenhouse, so more suitable to growing tomatoes. Always a great crowd, and it tends to be a quick-moving game on a cracking pitch or an absolute dustbowl. Maybe a contender for best food on the circuit, with bananas and custard on the menu daily.

Warwickshire

The new pavilion is massive, and on T20 finals day the atmosphere at Edgbaston is electric. But a

Championship game in front of 1,500 cold supporters dotted around the vast stands is not quite as exciting, in fact it can be pretty soulless. Biggest but coldest dressing-rooms on the circuit. I sometimes think they turn the air conditioning down to zero just to wind us up.

Worcestershire

New Road is what I'd call a proper county ground: good food, lovely supporters and nice comfy changing-rooms. I always love playing there and it's another place with top dressing-room attendants. A few years ago they installed a world-class coffee machine for the players which always takes a battering. The only thing which lets Worcester down are the hotels. Plenty of them, including one on the ground now, but I've never stayed in a decent one.

Yorkshire

Like one or two other places, I'm not sure how much the players were considered when they rebuilt the dressing-rooms. They are an improvement on the old ones under the rugby stand but the fact that the balcony had to be added after Dickie Bird apparently pointed out its omission says a lot. The changing-rooms are windowless and there would just about be enough room in the viewing area for the under-11s. Despite this, with all the history, Headingley is a good place to play and Leeds, with a big student population, means it's a lively spot and there are a couple of great chippies within walking distance. Not that I've ever visited them, of course.

12

When the Treadmill Stops

WHEN MY England ambitions ended, I had to accept that county cricket was going to be my lot. This is always a tough time in a player's career when the end is nearer than the beginning and thoughts (and a sense of panic) turn to life after cricket.

I have played for many years without the carrot of England selection, but that didn't mean my performances dipped. Some of my best years were when a selector wouldn't have even given me a second thought, but I take pride in the fact I still trained hard and put in as much, if not more work, than I did when I was climbing the ladder. It's the same for everyone who doesn't quite make it to the very top. You still feel you have something to prove, even if it's to yourself.

Mentally it gets tougher, though. To stay driven and focused over a long period of time takes a lot out of you which is when having a good coach helps, someone who recognises that as you get older your needs as an individual change and he or she adapts accordingly.

But I am also proud that I have made a conscious decision to try and give back to the game, to be a good role model for younger players. I know this is going to sound a bit clichéd, but I really do want to leave a legacy so that when I retire my old team-mates will say 'he always trained and practised hard. He had a good attitude to setbacks.' I think I have fulfilled that ambition. In fact, I know I have. Many of my team-mates and coaches have told me.

I also discovered that being a good team-mate and a bit of a role model can help keep you in the team for longer because once you stop scoring runs or taking wickets as consistently as you once did, you are forgotten about very quickly, sometimes within weeks of that decline starting.

In the 2020 season, if I did badly or was even out injured for a couple of weeks I could sense a different attitude among people at the club: 'Oh, he's struggling, he's on his way out.' Luckily, I had the support of a coach who probably knew I was on the decline but who still wanted to keep pushing me and make me as good as I could be at that stage of my career. After the career I'd had, he probably felt I deserved it. I know I did.

But the vultures do start circling more quickly. You are still doing the same things in terms of your preparation that you have done for the best part of two decades, but there's not the leeway given to a 21-year-old who is still learning about the game. You can't afford to make mistakes. True, as an older player you spot the hazards more quickly, you can second guess what people are thinking when you are struggling because you've seen so much.

Throughout my career I always batted in the top six, and a lot of time in the top four. And doing that role consistently is bloody difficult in England, certainly in red-ball cricket. Towards the end you start thinking about dropping down the order and having an easier time because, believe me, coming in at five or six when the ball is 80 overs old and bowlers are into their third spells is infinitely easier than facing the new ball and fresh bowlers when you haven't got a clue how the pitch is going to play. I genuinely believe for batsmen one of those slots between five and seven in the order is worth four or five runs to your average. Anyone who bats in the top four in English conditions consistently can easily slot into the middle order. Not many successfully do it the other way around. It is different in one-day cricket. Your main ambition is just to get in the team and stay there. Your role can evolve from that point.

When I think about it, I wonder how I'm the one still standing. A group of us played for England at age-group level before we became pros and most went on to have a decent county career, but I'm the only one playing now. It feels like it's a feather in my cap. How many players have I seen off? They tried to take me out, take my contract, take everything from me when I was an aspirational player. Then, when I had a good contract, a regular position in the team and a bit of a profile in the English game, there was a constant stream of people trying to take that away from me.

At the start you're hunting for the player you can take out and then you become the hunted. And in the middle ground you're also hunting; hunting England, hunting to be the best. But towards the end, and sorry to labour the hunter cliché here, but you can be a wounded animal with an injury. You quickly go from being a senior player to an old player, and it happens in an instant, like a switch being flicked. It is not a gradual process at all. A month of poor form, perhaps even less than that, and suddenly you're viewed differently. One minute you think you'll be playing forever and then you realise you only have a few games left.

Even when you come to accept that you are no longer first choice there is still pressure externally; you are always trying to prove yourself to someone even if it's not yourself: team-mates, coaches, selectors, family, people who watch. It goes back to that problem with cricket as opposed to other sports, everyone has an instant barometer of how you perform – your runs or your bowling analysis. In other team sports such as football, you can have a stinker and get substituted and if the team wins your shit performance is largely forgotten. Not so much in cricket. If you get nought everyone knows about it. If you get a run of low scores or stop taking wickets so the external pressure increases, and that's when it helps if you can keep a sense of perspective.

There's a group of us around the county circuit who text each other regularly if we make nought or get tonked all over the park. Obviously, the messages wouldn't start flying the moment it happened – we're not that hard-nosed – but we would console each other, although it was often tinged with black humour about the occasional absurdity of the situation. Everyone is on your back because you get nought, but only you and the umpire know that the lbw decision he gave was shit or that you could have taken four wickets instead of one if your team-mates could catch.

I haven't played a lot of second-team cricket in the back end of my career, but a couple of years ago I remember coming back from injury and a senior player I didn't know too well was playing for the opposition. He couldn't get in his county's red-ball team, but immediately gravitated towards me as a kindred spirit and we spent the next few hours grizzling together about our respective situations. There must be a collective noun to describe us: the has-beens or the once-weres, perhaps.

You still have bursts of inspiration and motivation, or if your team is doing well you get bowled along with the euphoria, but it gets harder and harder. The biggest driver is, of course, money. If you're still on over £70k and there's another year left on your contract, you're going to want to do it.

I talk about luck a lot because it plays such a big part in cricket. One area where I have been very fortunate is injuries. I've had a few things gone wrong but I've never missed a prolonged period of cricket, nothing more than a couple of months which, over nearly 20 years, is something I'm proud of.

But there's a difference between injury and being fit to play. I would say during my career the number of games I have played when there has been nothing physically wrong with me would be one in five at best. I can't remember the last season I started when I was at 100%. Most players, not necessarily all bowlers by the way, would say the same.

Pre-season is usually pretty intense. It's a new season so you're aware that you need to perform to keep your place. You push yourself and get injured. Players are always pretty fit by T20 time, though. We're into the rhythm of the season, we've done the hard yards and, of course, there is proper time between games to rest and we're not spending endless days and nights stuck behind the wheel or sleeping in uncomfortable beds.

It's not healthy to play through the pain barrier, to take injections just to get through a game but we all do it. And we all admire those team-mates who make those sacrifices, because they are usually the guys who are going to win the game for us. Others head to the treatment table at the first sign of a sprain. They don't usually have long careers.

So how can we have more time when we're bursting with energy during the season? Playing less is an obvious solution, but I can't see the fixture list shrinking any time soon. I've always thought we could extend the season a couple of weeks into October. The weather then tends to be much better than late March or early April. That would create some breathing space in the fixture list. Players would be happy to do that if it meant some more time for rest during the high months of the summer.

As I contemplate a future away from the game, one area where I feel so much more could be done is preparing for the transition from finishing your career and starting your next one. The first mention of 'retirement' or 'post-cricket' is as anxious as anything for players of a certain age. I believe clubs could do more to help players to deal with this big change in their life rather than always focusing on the performance side. It is a bit like school. You spend all your time learning Pythagoras or what an isosceles triangle is. What about how to get a mortgage, what insurance you need and what is the best way to save your money?

One really good initiative, introduced recently by the PCA and the counties, is the instigation of a sort-of retirement pot which gives every pro a lump sum, depending on his length of service, in the April after you retire, just at the time if you've packed up the previous September when you might be worrying a bit about the state of your finances. It's not a life-changing amount of money; it's roughly a year's salary but it's going to be a huge lift for me when the time comes.

The PCA are excellent, I don't think many players would disagree. They started with four regional development managers and now have one working with each county and they are always there when you need them. If I wanted them to, they'd call me every week. They help if you're in debt or if you're ill, but they're only as good as the funding they get. It's a tough balance for them, because they have to negotiate on our behalf and work with the ECB but be aware that the ECB also helps fund the PCA. But the benefits we get from PCA membership are second to none. The psychological and financial support, the sponsorship opportunities and the help they give when you think about or leave cricket are outstanding.

And when it's time to throw your last bit of kit at the posse of middle-aged men looking up expectantly towards the dressing-room balcony, what do you do next? I look at some of the guys I started with who retired a long time ago and the majority have moved into the finance sector. I can see the appeal. If you can commit yourself to training and learning for a couple of years the financial rewards will soon dwarf those you earned from cricket.

Personally, I won't be going into full-time coaching, but I can also see its attraction. Even if you've earned £80k in the last year of your playing contract a £40k-a-year job running the seconds has its appeal, not necessarily financially of course but as a way of getting your feet under the table. You're still in the game and if you are good at coaching you can carve out a little niche for yourself in an environment where there isn't much pressure and work towards something bigger. Me? I'd prefer to be on a banker's or an accountant's wage until I retire at 60!

But I will carry on playing. I made a commitment a few years ago when the time came I would go back and turn out for my club again on a regular basis. A lot of pros walk away from the game completely, but they tend to be the ones who leave under a bit of a cloud when their contract isn't renewed. I can understand that, but I think it is important to acknowledge those that allowed me to get where I am, a kid from state school who went on to play professional cricket. They will probably pay me a few quid but my plan is to plough all that money back into the club, whether it's to pay for the teas, improve the nets or help enable a couple of the juniors to take up a scholarship overseas.

If I'm shit and they have to drop me, then fair enough. Club cricket isn't doing to define me. I'm not going to go back there as some great saviour, but if I can help a young player bat in the top order and guide them through a season that will be enough for me.

When the time comes to step into the big wide world outside I won't have any regrets at all, and that's probably my biggest achievement. I've won domestic trophies, I played in front of big crowds, I've travelled the world, I've even written a book – I've had a great time. But the most important thing for me is, for all I have achieved as a player, when I finish playing I am sure people will rate me as a person, not a cricketer. They will look at the player I was and the way I treated other players, not the number of wickets I took or runs I made. I always played with a smile on my face, and I enjoyed every second of it. It's not a bad legacy for any English county cricketer's career, is it?

When we sit and reflect after we retire the one thing we realise is how lucky we have been, not just to play the game we love for a living but also for the support we get from our partners. It's hard. We're away a lot and we become acclimatised to living in hotels, where everything is done for you. Then, when you get home, you have to adjust. If you don't have a very understanding partner, the relationship will never work. It can be easy for players to think it's all about them and it's sometimes hard to remember partners are going through their own stuff.

If you've been away for a long period of time, you can feel like strangers when you see each other again, and even harder if you're only home for a week and then head off again. You're both under pressure, they will have their own careers but they have been home alone looking after the kids. Sometimes you're away so much your own home feels like an alien environment and your partner feels like they're a single parent.

My partner is amazing. She's supported me the whole way through my life in cricket. She's got her own career and has her own life and is highly successful in it, but she's never asked me not to go abroad or put pressure on me to be at home. It does help that she doesn't like cricket and never watches it, so it's always great for me to come home and for her to not care if I'd got nought or 100. I realise how fortunate I am in this regard. Every season I have played, in every dressing-room I have been in, there have always been at least a couple of break-ups. I'm amazed that there aren't more to be honest.

***

I wonder how I will feel if I pick this book up in, say, ten years and read it again. I hope that things do improve for the next generation of English pros, the guys making their way in county cricket. Maybe they will be paid more, maybe they will get longer contracts, maybe they will get more time to rest and recover between games. They might even be playing shorter games than 100 balls. You never know, they might have more room to get changed at Grace Road.

The likelihood is that none of that will happen, but it won't mean they can't have the time of their lives like those who came before them. I hope when they retire that they feel they have had the best of times, playing the greatest game in the world in front of people who mostly just want you to be successful.

For all its faults, county cricket is a wonderful thing which deserves to be cherished and nurtured. Of course, we can do things better, but as I write at the start of 2021 England are the best team in the world, judged across all formats of the game. Everyone involved in that success learnt their trade in county cricket and they have given so much pleasure to so many people in this country thanks to it. I think that's worth remembering.

You may read this as a follower of county cricket and not have the faintest idea who I am or where I played, but the game is only as good as the people who follow and watch it. You might think no one appreciates you, but trust me, as I look back on my career, it is the special blend of characters I see every day that I will remember and love when I tell my grandchildren about my career as an English county cricketer.